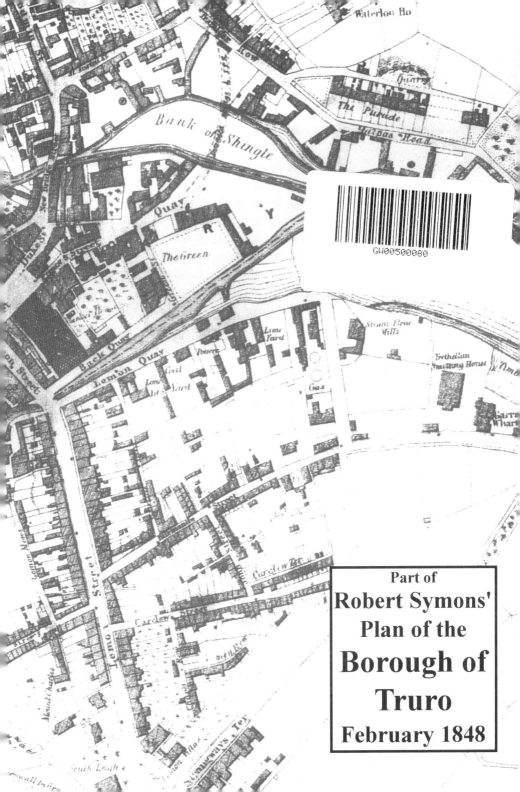

Part of
**Robert Symons'
Plan of the
Borough of
Truro**
February 1848

10th November '97.
an "Anniversary" to celebrate!
from Norma.

A HISTORY OF
TRURO

Viv Acton

Viv Acton

Viv was born Vivien Mary Law in Crediton, Devon, in 1939. Having attended Crediton High School, where she was Head Girl in 1957-8, she read History at Bristol University, was awarded an Honours Degree in 1961, and went on to teach History, first at Shute School near Axminster, and then at Hartley Wintney Secondary Modern (later Yateley Comprehensive) School in Hampshire. In 1968 she became Head of the large History Department at Yateley.

In 1973 marriage to Bob Acton (then teaching English) brought Viv to Cornwall. For two years (1975-7) she joined Bob at Falmouth School, and in 1978 took up a post at Truro High School, where she eventually became Head of History.

Viv retired from teaching in July 1991 in order to turn her attention to writing and sharing in the work of running the small publishing business Bob had by then set up. (Writing *chez* the Actons is a variation on the story of Jack Sprat and his wife: Viv vets Bob's attempts at writing local history, whilst he sees to her commas, colons and semicolons!)

Viv began by researching the fascinating history of the small community of Point and Penpol, near Devoran, where she and Bob live. The outcome was her first book, *Life by the Fal, Years of Change at Point and Penpol* (1993), which soon sold out and has recently (1997) been reprinted. In the next two years she worked with Derek Carter of Manaccan on two books about the little-known but very eventful history of World War 2 in Cornwall, producing two of Landfall's best-selling titles, *Operation Cornwall 1940-1944: The Fal, the Helford and D-Day* and *Cornish War and Peace: The Road to Victory - and Beyond*.

Since 1993 Viv has been working in a group, led by June Palmer, researching aspects of Truro's history, and she has contributed chapters to two books: *Edwardian Truro* (1994) and a forthcoming volume on the town's history in the years immediately preceding the accession of Queen Victoria. In 1995 she was commissioned by Truro High School to write a new history of the school to mark the centenary in 1996 of the school buildings, resulting in the publication of *High Days: Truro High School Celebrates*. From these researches arose a deeper interest in Truro, now bearing fruit in the form of the present book and in due course (we trust!) its successor.

VIV ACTON

A HISTORY OF
TRURO

Volume 1
From Coinage Town
to Cathedral City

**Landfall Publications
1997**

First published 1997
by
LANDFALL PUBLICATIONS
Landfall, Penpol, Devoran, Truro, Cornwall TR3 6NW
Telephone: 01872-862581

A CIP catalogue record for this book is available from the British Library.

ISBN
1 873443 33 1 (clothbound)
1 873443 34 X (paperback)

Printed by the Troutbeck Press
and bound by R.Booth Ltd., Antron Hill, Mabe, Penryn, Cornwall

Picture details
Front cover
Truro from Kenwyn Church, 1806 (detail)
Drawn by William Varley and engraved by F.C.Lewis
(The complete engraving is reproduced in black-and-white on page 4.)
Back cover
The west end of St Mary's church, seen from High Cross, 1824
Drawn by G.A.Moore and engraved by J.Greig
(from Stockdale's *Excursions through Cornwall*)
Page 224 and opposite page/inside back cover
A highly detailed engraving of Truro from Poltisco, a favourite viewpoint
for 19th century artists. This one can be dated between the late 1850s, when
the viaducts were completed, and 1862, when the first Boscawen Bridge was
replaced. The chimneys of three smelting works (Trethellan, Carvedras and
the Truro Smelting Works) can all be seen. A train is pulling in to the
station at Newham.
(Courtesy Royal Cornwall Polytechnic Society)

CONTENTS

IN PREPARATION

A HISTORY OF
TRURO
Volume 2
Cathedral City and County Town

Publication planned for late 1998

Foreword One

Being asked to write a foreword to a "history book" might suggest to some that you yourself belong to that history. This book concerns our yesterdays and certainly some of those yesterdays are mine.

Like Viv Acton I have been involved in trying to teach local history to Cornish children and, more particularly, with children in the town of Truro. Most of them respond to the problems and pleasures of their living background with an original, untaught enthusiasm, frequently surprising the teacher with approaches and reactions which have not occurred to their elders.

The history of a town should not be written for the child, but it should always have the children in mind, and be written so that they, their parents and their grandparents can all appreciate the life of their predecessors in it and the current of those centuries.

Occasionally a place is touched by national and international events, sometimes it throws up and out a character who gains more than local reputation, but usually it goes on its own sweet way. If there is a pattern to life within its boundaries it is of a struggle to survive disease and disaster in the attempt to achieve the accepted standard of "normality". The struggle can be leavened by looking towards Heaven and often by a variety of entertainment designed to prevent boredom.

Viv Acton has set herself a deliberate task, and, I think, she has performed it well.

H.L. Douch, former Curator of the County Museum, Truro

Truro in the middle of the nineteenth century. Here we see the mouth of the Kenwyn River, spanned by Lemon Bridge and flanked by Back Quay. On the left is the gas works. (Another detail from this engraving is on page 12.)

Foreword Two

Truro's past comes to life in this book. For the historian the facts have been widely researched and the references quoted, giving the book the authenticity required by the author's historical training. Building on this framework, Viv Acton sets the events in Truro in the context of what was happening at the time around the County, in England and overseas.

The present day City of Truro is full of fascinating hints of its past: in street names such as Old Bridge Street, Castle Street, St Dominic Street or Lemon Street; in grand houses such as Princes House and the Mansion House; in buildings like the Coinage Hall and the Assembly Rooms; in its quays and so on. Now these glimpses of the past are brought alive with the people, the environment, the way of living and the important events of each period.

The importance of the Charters to the development of the town is made clear, granting privileges and duties to the Mayor, Burgesses and Townspeople. Here we see the heritage that is in trust for the citizens of today.

This book will take you in to each page of Truro's history, living there, yet anxious to turn the page to move on in the story.

Richard Holloway

Richard Holloway, The Right Worshipful Mayor of Truro

The Coat of Arms of the City of Truro

Truro in the middle of the nineteenth century. This second detail from the engraving, the whole of which is reproduced on page 187, shows the mouth of the Allen River, crossed by the first Boscawen Bridge. On the far right is the Truro Tin Company smelting works. The chimney in the foreground may be the one that still stands beside Malpas Road, on the opposite side of the river from Tesco's.

Acknowledgements

My thanks to Angela Broome, Librarian of the Courtney Library,
Royal Institution of Cornwall (RIC);
Peter Gilson of the Royal Cornwall Polytechnic Society;
Roger Penhallurick of the RIC;
staff of the Cornwall Records Office (CRO),
the Cornish Studies Library, Redruth, and Truro City Library;
Jean Bennett; Sally Brocklehurst; David Brannlund;
Della & Don Curtis; Joyce Foster; Jenny Gason; Heather Haden;
Richard and Marion Holloway; Alex Hooper; John James;
Christopher Kingston; Richard Lingham; Bettie O'Neill;
Carol & Barry Simpson; Elizabeth Thompson.

Particular thanks to Leslie Douch, Joanna Mattingly and June Palmer
for reading the text and giving their help and advice.

This book is dedicated
to my husband Bob
for his help and encouragement.

Chapter 1

From Charter to Coinage

The origins of Truro are obscure. Truro is not mentioned in the Domesday Survey of 1086, and William I's commissioners had little to report on the manor of Trehaverne. For this manor on the western side of the River Allen, where the fresh waters of the river met the salt tides of the upper Fal estuary, they recorded one smallholder and one slave living on land worth only 12 pence. There was one acre of ploughland but no plough, and forty acres of pasture but no cattle or sheep. (One acre then represented perhaps 120 acres today so the lands were more extensive than would first appear.) The other manors nearby seemed far more desirable. Moresk on the east side of the Allen, mostly in the parish of St. Clement, was worth nearly £10 with cultivated land, pasture, woodland and farm animals, mainly sheep. To the south lay Goodern and Kea, each worth 10 shillings, and to the north was Allet, or Idless, worth 15 shillings, all with ploughland, woodland, pasture and animals.[1] But it was not in any of these wealthier manors, but in the southern part of the small manor of Trehaverne that the chartered borough of Truro began to emerge, because it was here that routeways met by land and sea.

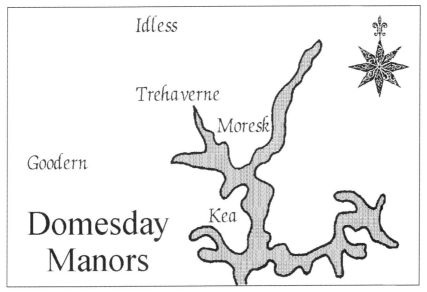

From Charter to Coinage

The tidal Truro river, on the upper reaches of the huge Fal estuary, brought sea-going boats far inland and in those days of difficult travel by land the water was a unifier not a divider. At the point where the rivers Kenwyn and Allen flow down to meet the tide a narrow triangle of land stretches out between them. Here these rivers were shallow enough to be forded at low tide, and one of the main routes east-west through Cornwall made use of this, so connecting this place with Penryn, Helston and Marazion to the south and west and Grampound, Liskeard and Calstock to the east. In addition the even more ancient route across Cornwall, from the Gannel estuary on the north coast, came down the shoulder of land that divided the two rivers into the centre of this triangle and so to the Fal estuary. This route connected Cornwall with Ireland and Wales to the north and with Brittany and other parts of Western Europe to the south. Truro, which grew up on this triangle hemmed in by the waters and steep hills, was therefore at the centre of trade routes.

Several explanations have been put forward for the meaning of the name of Truro. In the eighteenth century, Thomas Tonkin[2] suggested that the name came from *Tri*, three and *Ru*, roads, "the three principal streets" coming into Truro from the north, east and west. More recently H.L.Douch[3] has written: "I would suggest that the name *Tri-veru, Try-weru, Trywru* or *Tryurw* as it appears in documents of the thirteenth century was meant to convey to those who understood Cornish the equivalent of the English 'Three Rivers'", the three rivers being the Kenwyn, Allen and a little stream now running under Tregolls Road, which entered a creek, later infilled and now covered by the Trafalgar Square roundabout. Oliver Padel[4] disagrees with this suggestion and has tentatively suggested *people of the river crossing*. "This meaning would suit Truro very well, since the two river crossings are the significant feature of its location, but it is much harder to justify linguistically..." Whatever is the correct interpretation, these speculations all emphasise the importance of the routeways.

It was on the low land at the bottom of the hill down which the road came from the north coast and the administrative district of Pydar, that a tall granite cross was erected. Many wayside crosses were set up from the eleventh to the thirteenth centuries to mark tracks and footpaths to guide travellers to churches, monasteries and holy wells or to mark important routeways.[5] Although the first record of Truro's cross dates from 1290, when Truro was already an established borough town, this wheel-headed cross was probably far older, as indicated by the sharp angle made in the boundary of the burgage plots to accommodate it.[6]

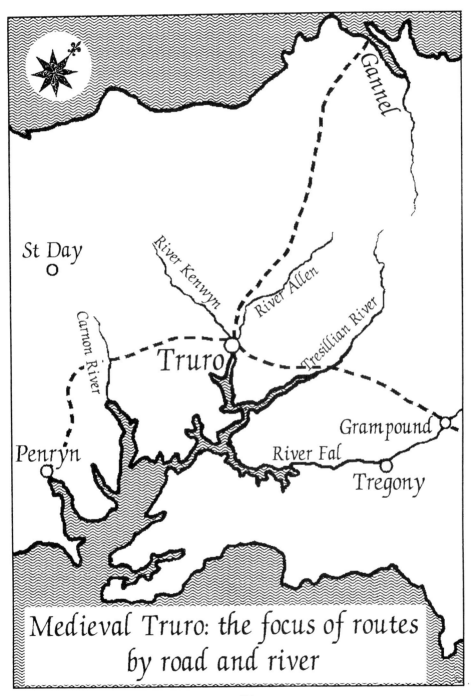

Medieval Truro: the focus of routes by road and river

The ancient wheel-headed cross which can be seen in High Cross today was discovered in 1958 by workmen digging a deep trench in St Nicholas Street. It was saved from destruction or re-burial by Mr Douch, the Curator of the County Museum, who realised its possible significance, and it has now been re-erected on a new shaft close to where it might have stood in earlier centuries.

This cross was probably already in place when a small castle was built on the hill above, strategically placed on the spur between the two rivers close to the ancient road from the north. Its origins are unknown but during the twelfth century a long-drawn-out battle for the throne broke out between two of the grandchildren of William the Conqueror, Matilda and Stephen. During these violent years many castles were built by barons embroiled in the fighting and it is thought that Truro's was one of them. Like Launceston Castle it was built on a circular mound. It had stone walls 3 feet thick and about 75 feet in diameter, constructed of local slate laid without cement, as was discovered about seven hundred years later in 1840, when the area was being levelled for a cattle market.[7] When Matilda's son, Henry II, became King in 1154 one of his first acts was to order the destruction of over one thousand of these strongholds, and again it is thought that this was the fate of Truro's castle.

The present Crown Court
(centre-right in this photograph by Paul Strings, 1992)
is built on or close to the site of the long-vanished Truro Castle.

Certainly by about 1270 it was described as a "placea", a vacant plot.[8] So having a castle might not have been a very important factor in Truro's growth, but for a town to have status it had to have a charter and it was usual for this to be first granted by the lord of the manor. These wars had brought into Cornwall in 1140 the man who was to be founder of the borough, Richard de Lucy, who was granted the manor of Tregavran (Trehaverne).

Richard de Lucy had been appointed Chief Justiciar by Stephen and was kept in this position when Matilda's son, Henry II, became King in 1154, so making him one of the most powerful men in the country. His main estates were in Essex but it was he who gave the embryo town of Truro its first charter. Its position at the centre of trade routes made it an ideal site to establish a market. We do not know for certain the details of Richard's arrangements for his market town, whether he created a completely new town out of part of his manor or whether he conferred a charter on an existing settlement, which perhaps seems the more likely. For a new town to succeed it had quickly to attract a number of skilled craftsmen such as tanners, shoemakers, weavers, smiths, masons, saddlers and bakers, so Richard probably encouraged people to settle here by the offer of the status of freeman for all those who took the new burgage plots carved out of the villeins' holdings. Local villeins might not possess the necessary skills[9] so people might have come from existing towns, such as Bodmin or Launceston, or perhaps it was foreigners who seized the opportunities offered.

Richard's charter, if it indeed existed in written form, is now lost, but a date of about 1153 has been suggested for it.[10] It seems to have given the townspeople the right to manage their own affairs: to have their own borough court, to hang their own thieves, and to have a weekly market and annual fair, where the tolls exacted could be very profitable to both the townspeople and their lord.

It was normal for such a charter to be confirmed by the King in due course, but in Cornwall at that time the support of another important man was also necessary. This was Reginald, Matilda's half-brother and the uncle of the new King, Henry II, who had earlier assumed the title Earl of Cornwall during the wars between Matilda and Stephen.[11] From a study of the witnesses, Reginald's charter for the new borough, later confirmed by the King, was granted possibly between 1161 and 1166.[12] It was addressed to both the Cornish and the English Barons of Cornwall and refers to the "free Burgesses of Triueru". It confirmed the privileges granted to them by Richard de Lucy and it also gave them some extra ones. These included freedom from paying tolls in any other

From Charter to Coinage

Cornish market, and freedom from the jurisdiction of the county court and the courts of the smaller administrative districts of the hundreds.[13] This would make it less likely for Truro men to get involved in disputed contracts, or unpaid debts, or breaches of market regulations which could be costly and lengthy.[14] This document is still in existence, the oldest town charter to survive in Cornwall and one of the oldest in the country.

Facsimile of the earliest surviving charter of the Borough of Truro
(from A Trade & General Directory of the City of Truro, 1880, courtesy
Cornish Studies Library, Redruth)

Translation: Reginald the King's son Earl of Cornwall to all Barons of Cornwall and all Knights and all free Tenants, and all persons as well English as Cornish Greeting. - Know ye that I have granted to my free Burgesses of Truro to have all free customs and Town Rights and the same in all things which they had in the time of Richard de Luci (to wit) sac and soc and toll and them and Infangtheof*. And I have granted to them they they shall not be impleaded in the Hundred nor in the County Courts nor shall go for any summons to plead elsewhere without the Town of Truro. And that they shall be quit from paying toll throughout all Cornwall in Fairs and in Markets and wheresoever they shall buy or sell, and that for money owing to them and not paid they may take a Distress in their Town from their Debtors. These being Witnesses Roger de Valletort, Robert de Dunstanville, Richard de Roddona, Aluredas de Saint Martin, and very many others at Tiverton.

* "sac ... Infangtheof": "Anglo-Saxon words of vague meaning but implying the right to regard themselves as a separate community, to have a court of their own, hang their own thieves and, in general, manage their own affairs without the interference of the officials of the manor out of which the borough had grown." (Charles Henderson, *Essays in Cornish History*)

Some time after the 1220s when the new orders of friars were looking for towns to establish themselves in Cornwall, the Franciscans, the grey friars, settled in the largest town, Bodmin, but the Dominicans, the black friars, did not choose Launceston or Liskeard as might have been expected: they came further west to Truro. Unlike the wealthier monastic orders the friars did not build large self-contained precincts, but often established themselves in poorer areas of a town or in its suburbs from where they set out to preach in the market place and in the villages, depending on local good will for their food. The black friars acquired land on the western outskirts of Truro, close to the ford over the Kenwyn river. The name "St Dominic Street" recalls their presence today and perhaps marks what was the western limit of their property. The eastern limit was probably near what is now Victoria Square opposite the bottom of Calenick Street, according to a rental of 1407-8.[15] Many years later, in Henry VIII's reign, a plan of the south coast of Cornwall showed the friary's church as having a tall tower with pinnacles, but this might just have been the artist's imagination.[16] If the three bells that were recorded in 1538 were already in place on 29 September 1259, their clashing jangle would no doubt have echoed over the roofs of the little town to welcome the Bishop of Exeter when he came to consecrate their new church.

Bishop Bronescombe's visit was a very significant event for Truro. Not only was such a visit rare because of the long and difficult journey from Exeter, but there were three churches for him to consecrate in the immediate area. His first stop, on 27 September, was to the "Church of Keynewn", Truro's parish church, built high up on the hill overlooking the small town. Here the solemn ritual would have been enacted of the blessing and sprinkling of holy water, followed by the celebration of the eucharist and then the enclosure of consecrated bread and wine inside the altar.[17]

After this ceremony the townspeople would have trooped back to the town, passing the sinister cross beams of the town's gallows where sometimes the body of a thief was to be seen slowly swinging.[18] (The name of Comprigney Hill probably comes from the Cornish word *cloghprennyer*, meaning bell beams or gallows.) There, close to the ancient High Cross, the final preparations would be made to welcome the bishop the following day for the dedication of their chapel of St Mary. The bishop's blessing of the chapel was important for Truro people. Not only might it save them the uphill walk to Kenwyn church, particularly tiring for the very young and the very old, but it was another sign of the growth of this small town and yet one more step towards greater independence. Kenwyn church would remain their parish church for a little longer, where they would still gather on Sundays and feast days, but now their own town chapel would have official sanction for daily masses.

During these years Truro men had to fight to maintain and enhance their privileged position. Their monopoly of the trade on the Fal was already being threatened by Penryn, whose market had been established by another bishop in 1236. Six years after the consecration of St Mary's chapel in Truro Bishop Bronescombe would have passed through the town again on the way to Penryn to lay the foundation stone of Glasney College. This new foundation not only gave protection to Penryn, which was to become the second most important town on the estuary of the Fal, but it also gained control over the major tithes of the churches of Kenwyn and Kea. It might have been at this time that the chapel of St Mary became a parish church in its own right with its own rector, John de Belsal, who was installed during the year 1264-5. The area of the parish was small, consisting only of the triangle of land between the rivers Allen and Kenwyn, so that the two suburbs on the far side of these rivers remained in the parishes of St Clement and Kenwyn respectively. In 1288 "ecclesia de Treveru was valued at 4s 4d, being by far the poorest endowed benefice in the deanery of Powder."[19]

Immediately to the south of Truro was the settlement of Newham, whose name indicates its Saxon origins. The lord of this manor, Reginald de Pridias (Prydyas, Prydas, or Prideaux), wanted to develop a market on his own land, which would be a more immediate threat to Truro's monopoly in the area. He was possibly the first Lord of Newham, who was asserting his powers in his new property.[20] In 1262 the Truro men took their case to law, which meant travelling to Launceston when the royal judge was holding an Assize Court there, which was as far into Cornwall as the judges would usually go on their official circuits because of the poor state of the roads. The judge decided in favour of the Truro men: Reginald had to give up his claim to a meat and cloth market and Newham people could only buy or sell according to the assize and King's measure of Truro.[21]

Not all problems went to court as they arose. Powerful lords often tried to take the law into their own hands and settle quarrels by force. This happened in 1274 at Lanner, near Idless, on the manor of Cargoll which Bishop Bronescombe had recently acquired. He enclosed land there for a deer park, thus antagonising Edmund Earl of Cornwall, who jealously guarded what he felt was his sole right in Cornwall. The King, however, had earlier sold "the right of free warren" to many people and the bishop had been amongst the buyers. Some of the Earl's men came to Lanner and ripped up the new park fences. When the bishop's men tried to stop them they fought them, wounding the horse of a former Archdeacon of Cornwall. The bishop used the power of the church against these men by excommunicating them, that is cutting them off from all the benefits of the church, a terrible punishment at this time. However, even he dared not do this to the earl himself, who was the king's nephew. The quarrel must have simmered on and Truro became involved when the civil law was eventually brought into the matter. In the Assizes of 1283 it was said that this deer park obstructed the public highway leading to the market in Truro. When it was shown that a new road had been made to overcome the problem, however, the matter was resolved in the bishop's favour.[22]

At the same Assizes Truro's right to try and hang thieves was questioned by the judges after two local men had been caught red handed in Truro with stolen horses. The Truro Borough Court had dealt with them in the usual method and they had been hanged on the town gallows. The Burgesses had to prove that they had the right to do this by producing their two charters from Earl Reginald and Henry II.[23] This showed how important these deeds could be to protect the privileges of a town. These charters were already over one hundred years old and perhaps because of this, shortly afterwards the Burgesses had their charter confirmed by the reigning King at the time, Edward I. In June 1985, Truro was *en fête* to celebrate the seven hundredth centenary of the granting of this charter.

The Sunshine Charter!

THE PEOPLE of Truro took several steps back in time in Saturday's warm sunshine when they re-lived a moment 700 years ago when Edward I granted the town a charter.

For anyone who did a "double-take" when they saw people in Medieval dress as they went about their weekend shopping in Boscawen-street all was made clear when the Mayor of Truro, the Rev. Douglas Robins, stepped on to a raised wooden platform and declared the city's charter festivities begun.

A symbolic white glove was raised on a piece of thread to a Town Hall window. Counteracting the tradition of throwing down the gauntlet, the glove declared hostilities over and heralded the start of two days of fun.

People celebrated in a variety of ways. Two hundred children did it energetically when they took part in sports competitions at the Dreadnought playing field watched over by Queen Elizabeth I, alias Lorrie Eathorne. Others windsurfed, while some approached the festivities in a more leisurely fashion, sitting in the sun listening to Truro City Band and watching maypole dancers, or attending a family variety concert in the City Hall on Saturday evening.

Some celebrated in style, but others preferred none — like the entrants in Sunday's raft race who spent most of the time covered in either soot, flour, sand or mud.

But it was the "Clerical Errors", a team from Cornwall County Council clerks' department, who took the prize for the most entertaining raft. The strength of their performance lay in the way they had sabotaged most other craft before the race had even started.

While the raft race and other Barbarian activities went on, a civic procession to Truro Cathedral was being led by the Mayor. With him were the Bishop of Truro, the Rt. Rev. Peter Mumford; the Bishop of St. Germans, the Rt. Rev. Brother Michael, and councillors and magistrates.

(From the West Briton, *June 1985)*

24

Some felons might escape the gallows if they gained the sanctuary of St Mary's church and two such cases were reported at these Assizes. One was a thief who stole the strong-box of a Truro man, Peter le Normand, who then chased him through the streets until he gained the safety of the church. The other was a murderer, who killed a man in Dunmere Woods near Bodmin, and finally sought the sanctuary of St Mary's. They could not stay in the church indefinitely. The law stated that a criminal had a choice of either submitting to a trial or confessing the crime to the Coroner and then leaving the kingdom. If he refused to do this after forty days he would be starved into surrender. In both these cases the criminals confessed and left the country.[24] (There were certain places where a fugitive could stay in sanctuary for ever unpunished because no coroner was allowed to enter. Padstow was one such place and in later years a Truro man, Stephen Langhare, who it was alleged "cowardly and shamefully morderyed and wilfully slewe William Hoskyn", fled justice in this way.[25])

The same Assizes in 1283 also had records of two other cases of murder in Truro. One was the particularly unpleasant case of Ralph Hulkeman, who beat his wife, Agnes, so viciously that she died five days later. He had fled and the court declared him outlawed, so his goods and property were forfeit. The other case concerned Ralph de Bloyou, the head of an influential family near Marazion, who became involved in a furious disagreement with Joel the Glover in Truro. Ralph hit Joel so hard with the pommel of his sword that he later died. He escaped punishment on this occasion because he was able to produce the king's pardon for the crime, but the twelve jurymen who represented Truro at the Assizes were ordered to be put in prison for concealing the felony. They avoided this when their two spokesmen, Henry Maynard and David the Merchant, offered to pay a fine of 100s. This was not the end of the affair for Ralph, because some years later he was brought before the Judge again for the same murder, and this time no pardon was mentioned, and he refused to plead. This was a brave move on his part because if he had failed in his plea all his lands and goods would have been forfeit, so his family would have suffered. Instead he let justice take its course; being pressed by heavy weights until he pleaded or died.[26]

In about 1300 part of the lordship of Truro was sold to Thomas de Pridias, who was already Lord of Newham, and he was soon causing even more trouble than had his father Reginald. Thomas imprisoned Clarice, the wife of a prominent townsman, Robert Maynard, for apparently no better reason than that she had refused to give him a particular brooch, which must have been rather special as it was worth 40 shillings. He kept her in irons until she handed it over. On another occasion he terrified the people of Truro and the neighbourhood on market day by marching in with armed soldiers to look for and beat up another local lord. Robert Brison was later beaten and wounded by Thomas's men because he refused to sell them a garment for the price they offered. Their threats frightened him so much that he fled abroad until a friend had paid a 100-shilling fine for his presumption.

Not surprisingly the Truro Burgesses finally took these grievances to the Assizes in 1305, where Thomas retaliated by complaining that Truro people had broken into his deer park and stolen four fallow deer. The quarrel over power in the town was finally settled two years later, leaving Truro men in control of their own affairs, but the lord was to have the profits from the annual fair.[27]

A fraternity or guild, dedicated to St Nicholas who was the patron saint of sailors and sea-going merchants, was recorded in Truro in 1278. The historian Charles Henderson suggested that this was a guild of merchants who controlled the running of the town in the early years and whose guildhall became the meeting place for the town burgesses. This guild, however, is not mentioned in the early charters, and it may have been a religious one. If so this is the earliest religious guild so far discovered in Cornwall. Such organisations often undertook some responsibility for the church, perhaps the repair of the fabric, providing vestments, maintaining a side-chapel or a lighted candle before the image of their saint.[28] This guild or fraternity perhaps had its own chapel and cemetery situated where nowadays Lemon Street joins Boscawen Street. It gave its name to the street which then ran from the crossing of the Kenwyn River (Victoria Square) and extended along what is now the south side of Boscawen Street. St Nicholas Street, now much shorter, bears probably the oldest street name in the city today. (When the old King's Head Inn was being demolished at the end of the eighteenth century to connect the bottom of Lemon Street with the centre of the town, a panelled room with an arched window and carvings of the Apostles was taken down, and buried human bones were found nearby.[29] It is possible that this was the chapel and cemetery for the Guild of St Nicholas.)

During the last part of the thirteenth century Truro's importance was growing. The borough was represented in Parliament by two members, one of five boroughs in the county to hold elections for Edward I's Parliament in 1295, the first one for which all the names are recorded. (The other four boroughs at this time were Bodmin, Launceston, Liskeard and Tregony.) The two Truro men were Henry le Bailly and Robert Maynard, the latter probably being the husband of the wrongly-imprisoned Clarice. MPs did not have the same powers as now; they were mainly needed by the kings to endorse taxation and to help in its collection. The difficulties of travel could make their office a burden rather than a privilege, and sometimes the boroughs shared MPs possibly because of the expenses involved; they had to pay them 2s for each day that Parliament was in session as well as for the time spent in travelling.

Parliaments were called irregularly whenever the King felt the need for one, and met wherever the King happened to be at the time, not always in London. In 1332, for example, Truro's MPs, John de Cornwall and William Nevill, had to travel as far as Lincoln. John was a member of an important family, possibly descended illegitimately from Richard Earl of Cornwall, brother of Henry III. In spite of his position, or perhaps because of it, he seems to have had little respect for the law. Four years earlier there had been a complaint from a man in Oxfordshire that Richard de Cornwall with his two sons William and John had broken into his house, assaulted him, felled his trees, taken fish from his ponds and stolen horses, oxen, cows, sheep and swine worth £100.[30]

Several of Truro's early MPs were connected with the tin trade: both Henry le Bailly and Robert Maynard were recorded in the Stannary Rolls. It was merchants like them who were amongst the most important men in the town and Truro's prosperity was increasingly dependent on Cornish tin. In 1265 the King, Henry III, had sent Letters Patent to the Mayors of the French towns of Bordeaux and La Rochelle "to receive and treat well the Burgesses of Helston, Truro and Bodmin when they come thither with tin...or with other merchandise."[31] Although in the earlier years of the Middle Ages French or Italian ships carried most of England's exports, this document shows that ships from Cornwall also crossed the Channel. The importance of trade for Truro is indicated by the earliest seals granted to the new borough showing a one-masted ship with fore and aft castles, and fish in the sea below its keel.[32]

Medieval ports were usually not on the coast but situated higher up tidal rivers or creeks: both Truro and Penryn are examples. This had two main advantages: they were not so vulnerable to enemy attack and the overland travel distances could be reduced. There could be disadvantages, however, if the silting up of rivers was a problem. Tregony, higher up the Fal, was one of those boroughs important enough to be represented in Parliament in 1295, but when the river began silting up its days as a thriving port were over and it was Truro and Penryn that gained the advantage. Sea-going vessels were small - ships of 200 tons were considered large at that time - so the Truro river could easily accommodate them. The chief national exports were wool, lead and tin, and tin came almost exclusively from Cornwall and Devon, making it Europe's main source for this important metal during the earlier years of the Middle Ages.

From the early thirteenth century tin production in Cornwall increased from perhaps 100 tons in 1213 to over seven times that amount by the 1330s.[33] One of the reasons for this was an increase in demand, with tin being a basic material for both pewter and bronze. Pewter was used for jugs and tableware by those who could afford it in preference to wood, earthenware or leather. Bronze was used for church bells, which became increasingly popular, and then, as weapons of war became more destructive in later years, bronze was needed for cannons. As production increased so too did the need to control and administer this source of wealth and Truro was one of the towns to gain from this.

After the tin was extracted by streaming or openwork mining, the ore was smelted using crude kilns or simple blowing houses, usually situated near the place of production. The heavy ingots were then taken to be tested for quality before they could be sold through the official outlet, the staple. The testing process was called coinage because a corner (*coin* in French) was cut off each ingot and weighed and if up to standard the ingot was then given the official stamp. In 1305 84% of all the tin produced in Cornwall came from the eastern half of the county, but in that year tin ingots were stamped in Truro because, by a charter of Edward III, it was chosen with Lostwithiel, Bodmin, Liskeard and Helston, to be one of the towns to be used for the coinage of tin.[34] Truro's connection with the tin industry began in fact much earlier, because between Truro and the north coast was the stannary of Tywarnhayle, an area rich in tin, which was one of four established in the county, and a stannary court would frequently meet in the town to deal with any problems and arguments of the tinners of this area. In 1305 thirty-eight people's names were recorded in connection with the tin industry in the Truro area.[35]

The Earls of Cornwall had made Lostwithiel their headquarters for administration in the thirteenth century and it had been named as the only town where the tin could be sold but in 1327, in spite of protests from the people of Lostwithiel, the King issued a proclamation that the staple for tin in Cornwall should be held at Truro as well as Lostwithiel. Twenty-four years later the steward for the new Duchy of Cornwall was ordered to build or buy a house in Truro for coinage and this Duchy building was established at the east end of what is now Boscawen Street. (The Tudor-looking building with steep gable ends standing there today was built in the mid-nineteenth century on the site of the old Coinage Hall after that system finally ended in 1838.) For much of the fourteenth century, Lostwithiel still coined more tin than Truro, but it was these two places that were the regular coinage towns.[36]

The old Coinage Hall before its removal in 1847
(from A Remembrance of Truro *in the Bishop's Library)*

Coinages were usually held twice yearly, at Easter (later changed to Midsummer) and Michaelmas. The smelted tin was carried by trains of sturdy packhorses winding their way down the hills, splashing through the fords or clopping over the bridges into the town and so on to the Coinage Hall. There the heavy ingots, stamped with their smelters' mark, would be piled up to wait for the assayer's attention. The two main officials, the controller and receiver, would arrive at the Coinage Hall on the appointed day carrying the stamping hammer and weights in a sealed bag, where they met with the assay master and weigher and where the porters would be ready to move the heavy blocks of tin. "An open space was roped off in front, the King's beam was brought out and rectified by the controller and weigher, the weights were solemnly unsealed and handed to the weigher, the assay master made ready his hammer and chisels and the steward, controller and receiver took their seats facing the beam."[37] Then at noon, watched by the tinners, merchants and pewterers who had gathered in the Hall, the first ingots were weighed. With each block the weight was shouted out and recorded, then it was carried over to the assay master who chiselled off a small piece from the corner and assayed it for its quality. If it passed his inspection, the controller using the hammer stamped upon it the arms of the duchy. The whole process could be very time-consuming, no doubt bringing good business to Truro's inns, ale houses, shops and market stalls.

With such restrictions on the tin trade it is not surprising that some of the smelted tin never went through the official channels. There were smuggling specialists in the ports on the south coast, and no doubt they were not unknown in Truro. They converted tin that had not been coined into small blocks of "pocket tin" that were light enough and small enough to be easily carried and hidden. These were smuggled aboard ships or sold to travelling pewterers.[38]

By the mid-fourteenth century Truro had established itself as one of the main towns of Cornwall. In 1334, when a tax assessment was made trying to reflect the true wealth of the lay inhabitants, Truro's assessment was the second highest in the county, 161s, in between Bodmin (266s) and Lostwithiel (116s),[39] and it had more independence than these two towns, which were still under the power of the church or a lord. Truro was becoming increasingly wealthy and increasingly populous, but for all this by our standards today it was little more than a large village, where the fields were only a short distance from the quays and the High Cross on the hillsides above the town.

Each of the burgage properties, belonging to the wealthier people, had long plots of land stretching down on either side of Pydar Street to the banks of one or other of the two rivers. A house, probably with a shop and workroom, would be built beside the street, behind which would be space for storerooms, gardens and orchards or later building development. The Burgesses also had strips, or stitches, of land in the open fields of Trehaverne, Gweal Clogh Prennyer (Comprigney) and Gweal An Castel.[40] (*Gweal* is Cornish for an open, arable field.) Here in the early spring plough teams of oxen would be seen slowly plodding up and down. Men would then walk over the shallow furrows carrying large bags or baskets from which they broadcast the seed. In due time the harvest would be gathered: the corn cut with a swishing rhythm of scythes or sickles, the sheaves stacked and then the fields gleaned of the last remnants of the harvest. This was probably a community effort with men, women and children all playing their part. The farming season was part of the way of life of the townsmen.

The two rivers provided power for the corn mills, which were built at intervals along the valleys. The town mill was near the Kenwyn river, close to the western ford into the town, powered by a leat which was taken off from the river higher up the valley and then flowed back into it just past the mill. This leat, later called Tregeare Water, can be appreciated today as there is an attractive walk between it and the river coming almost into the heart of the city, although the last part of the leat has now been covered over.

The leat taken from the River Kenwyn, no longer used for commercial purposes, now provides an attractive walk in the heart of the City.
(Photograph by John James)

Millpool plan by Civic Society

A MODIFIED scheme for the improvement of Truro's Millpool is likely to be carried out as a Manpower Services Commission project.

Capt. John Whitehouse, Carrick Council's maritime officer, reported to the council's amenities committee last week that he had met representatives of Truro Civic Society, who had objected to the council scheme.

The Society, said Capt. Whitehouse, had drawn up a modified scheme which preserved the pool effect.

"I think this has a lot of merit in it and if we adopt it, its Civic Society will withdraw their objection," said Capt. Whitehouse.

The MSC, he said, would like to carry out the scheme

The committee decided to recommend the council to accept the Civic Society scheme.

Higher up the Kenwyn at Carvedras was the mill for the friary powered by another leat. The manorial mill was built on the Allen river just behind St Mary's church and the much reduced mill pool today is a reminder of it. (On the left is an article about it, taken from the *West Briton* of May 1985.) Not far away but a little higher up the river was the Duchy mill for the manor of Moresk.[41] Here there was a leat, now dried up, which then flowed back into the river nearby. Horses or lumbering oxen would be used to bring supplies of corn and flour to and from these mills, whose water wheels would continually creak and slosh as they turned the massive grinding stones inside.

On the east bank of the River Allen, near its confluence with the Truro river, was a field called Park Oxenford, close to the lowest ford over the river. This

31

ford was discovered in the mid-nineteenth century when excavations for new public rooms being built in Quay Street uncovered a track paved with sea pebbles leading down to the river. There were possibly three other fords over this river. The highest one crossed the river where Moresk bridge is today and from where a street, once known as Godynstret[42] and later as Goody or Goodwives Lane, led up the hill to the site of the castle. Two other fords in between them would have been where Old Bridge Street and New Bridge Street now cross the river.[43] The building of bridges was not always welcomed in the Middle Ages because they could stop the passage of ships, although the humped backs of the stone ones might allow small boats to negotiate the narrow archways.

The first bridge to be built here was probably in the early fourteenth century, known as the East Bridge (Old Bridge Street). From the East Bridge the road would have led past the church and on to the open space around the High Cross where stalls would probably be set out on market days. A bridge over the Kenwyn river, the West Bridge (where Victoria Square is today), was built at about the same time, and as late as the eighteenth century this, or its successor, was still remembered as being a narrow footbridge, perhaps wide enough for pack horses, with a ford and stepping stones beside it.[44]

The road into the town approached this bridge down a steep hill now known as Chapel Hill. Part way up this hill, out of the town but close enough not to be ignored, was the leper house built, as many were, beside the main road where travellers could be accosted for alms. Leprosy was quite common at this time, reaching a peak in the early fourteenth century, and it was a disease that was particularly dreaded because the mutilations caused by it could look horrific. Fingers and toes could slowly rot away as could noses and other facial features, and when gangrene set in there would be a terrible stink. A decree from the Pope in 1179 ordered lepers to live segregated from healthy people, and so special houses were built for them.[45] At Launceston lepers would be punished by the forfeit of their upper garment if they were found within the town[46] and perhaps Truro had the same rule. When Thomas Bytton, Bishop of Exeter, died in 1307, the time when the disease was perhaps at its worst, he left money to be distributed to the lepers of the diocese, and the Truro house received 12s from his executors.

At the bottom of the hill the road became Street Kenwyn, which passed by the walls of the friary with its main gate facing towards the West Bridge, the entrance into the town. We can only speculate about the layout of the town and its appearance at this time for much is not known and buildings that we do know existed have been pulled down by later generations. Close to the bridge, where St Nicholas Street began, the waters of the leat joined the Kenwyn where the mill wheel for the town mill busily clacked away. St Nicholas Street then continued past a building known as An' Hell (the Hall). (Charles Henderson suggested that this might have been the original Lord's Hall where the meetings of the Borough Court would have been held under the presidency of the Lord's steward, and which might have been later used as the town hall.) St Nicholas Street then followed the course of the south side of the present-day Boscawen Street, past the Guildhall and Chapel of St. Nicholas and so on to the Coinage Hall. This road may well have been on a ridge of higher ground between the two rivers standing above the mudflats that would be subject to flooding.[47] The most important quay at this time is thought to have been Back Quay on the Kenwyn,[48] but there may have been other small ones in addition to this. Linking the rivers and the streets would be small alleyways or opes, narrow, smelly and dark. Several of these still exist, such as the aptly named Squeezeguts Alley and Cathedral Lane, or Church Lane as it was once called amongst other names, but this one, with its summer floral decorations today, might give us a more attractive picture of a medieval lane than is warranted.

Besides the twice-yearly activity at the Duchy Coinage Hall, the two main areas of bustle and movement would be on the quays and in the market place. With the full tides, the arrival and departure of vessels to and from Brittany, Ireland, France, the Iberian Peninsula or from the coastal trade, would

Cathedral Lane today, formerly Church Lane,
and before that Narrow Street or earlier versions of the same,
such as Street Idden, Street Eden and Strethyn

34

bring flurries of activity; cargoes would be man-handled on and off board, perhaps tin, hides and coarse Cornish cloth for export, and salt or French or Iberian wines coming into the port. The weekly market, then as later, would bring local country people streaming into the town with their animals and produce. This market would serve a wide area and its importance is shown by the town's sometimes being referred to as Truro Marche. The market area in towns was usually large to accommodate animals and stalls, but the entrances were narrow to control entry and to make the collection of tolls easier,[49] and this could well have applied to the area around High Cross. The most important properties would be close to it, so it is likely that besides the burgage holdings on either side of Pydar Street, there would have been other burgage tenements on the south side, where artisans could display their goods from their properties that were workplace, shop and living quarters, all under one roof.

The time of greatest excitement during the year would be for the annual fair. Fairs were usually held in the summer when travel was easier and weather more clement, but Truro's fair was in November, and may have been connected with the feast of St. Martin. In the eighteenth century it became known as the Bullock and Beast Fair; in the Middle Ages, when farming practices did not allow for the growing of much winter fodder for cattle and other farm animals, many were slaughtered in the autumn and the meat heavily salted to preserve it for as long as possible. Perhaps this November fair brought animals to the market before the final slaughter. A glove would be erected by the High Cross to signal the opening and the whole area would be filled with people determined to gain as much profit as they could and to enjoy a last fling before the coming hard months of winter.

This would bring in people from much further afield and would be a time not only of buying and selling, sometimes exotic foreign goods, but also for people to pay rent or conduct other business. A document of 1280, granting a stitch of land stretching down to the River Allen to Margery, widow of William of Bosvisack, stipulated that she should pay a rent of 6d a year in three equal portions, the third part to be paid at Truro fair.[50] Crowds would attract the sellers of food and drink, so pies (pasties perhaps) would draw people to the stalls with appetising smells. Ale would be in great demand, although one sixteenth-century writer, Andrew Boorde, later described the Cornish variety as looking "whyte and thycke as if pygges had wrasteled in it".[51] Crowds would also be a magnet for wandering entertainers, such as jugglers, acrobats, ballad sellers and minstrels. Wrestling matches were no doubt held, with honour and prizes at stake.

From Charter to Coinage

High Cross still provides a focus for City events

The picture that emerges is of a small town, fighting successfully for its privileges, and prospering as a port, market and coinage town during the thirteenth and earlier fourteenth centuries, which was a time of growth for the country as a whole. A darker picture is to follow with the depredations of pestilence and war.

References

[1] Thorn, C. & F. (eds), *Domesday Book* 10: Cornwall (Phillimore, 1979)
[2] Quoted by Polsue.
[3] Douch, 1977
[4] Padel, 1988
[5] Langdon, Andrew, *Cornish Crosses*
[6] Truro Buildings Research Group, *Pydar Street & the High Cross Area,* 1975
[7] Whitley, H.M., "Notes on the History of Truro", JRIC X
[8] Henderson, 1963
[9] Beresford, 1988
[10] Sheppard, 1980
[11] Elliott-Binns, 1955
[12] Hull, Peter: "Truro's Proud Heritage", *West Briton Argus*, 13 May 1985
[13] Henderson, 1963
[14] Beresford, 1988

[15] Personal communication, Dr Joanna Mattingly

[16] Whitley, H.M., "The Dominican Friary", JRIC Volume VIII

[17] Orme, 1996

[18] Douch, 1977

[19] Henderson, C., JRIC 1960

[20] Personal communication, Joyce Foster

[21] Henderson, 1963

[22] ibid.

[23] ibid.

[24] Henderson, 1929

[25] Henderson MS, n.d.

[26] Henderson (Journal)

[27] Henderson, 1963

[28] Mattingly, J., Article in JRIC, 1989

[29] Henderson MS, n.d.

[30] Jennings, P., JRIC XIII

[31] Douch, 1977

[32] Dorling, 1982

[33] Hatcher, 1970

[34] Buck, Colin, *Walks Around Lostwithiel*, Lostwithiel Town Council, n.d.

[35] Jennings, P., JRIC XV

[36] Hatcher, 1970

[37] Pennington, 1973

[38] Halliday, 1959

[39] Beresford, 1988

[40] Douch, 1977

[41] ibid.

[42] Personal communication, Dr J.Mattingly

[43] Douch, 1977

[44] ibid.

[45] Gottfried, R.S., *The Black Death*, Robert Hale, 1984

[46] Orme, N. & Webster, M., *The English Hospital*, Yale University, 1995

[47] *Archaeological Investigations at City Hall, Truro, 1996*, CAU for The Hall for Cornwall Trust

[48] Sheppard, 1980

[49] Hindle,B.P., *Medieval Town Plans*, Shire Archaeology, 1990

[50] Henderson, Journal, 1929

[51] Nance, R. Morton, "Andrew Boorde on Cornwall", JRIC 1928

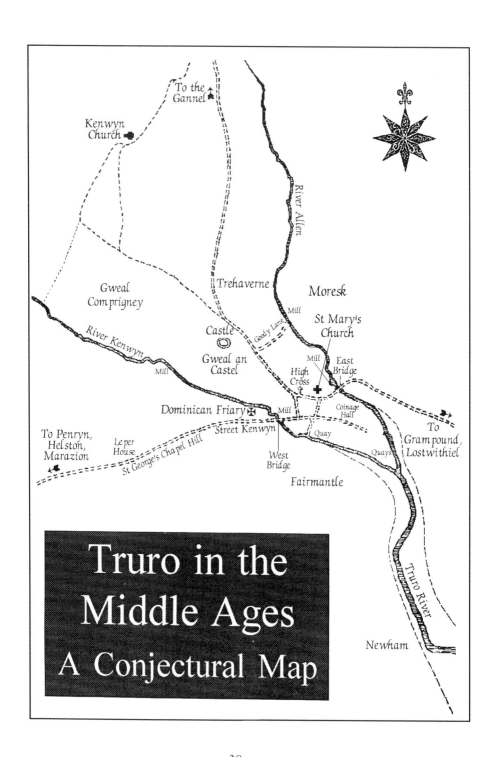

To the
Gannel

Kenwyn
Church

River Allen

Gweal
Comprigney

Trehaverne

Moresk

Mill

St Mary's
Church

River Kenwyn

Castle

Goody Lane

Gweal an
Castel

Mill

Mill

East
Bridge

High
Cross

Mill

Dominican Friary

Mill

Coinage
Hall

To Penryn,
Helston,
Marazion

Leper
House

St George's Chapel Hill

Street Kenwyn

Quay

Quays

To
Grampound,
Lostwithiel

West
Bridge

Fairmantle

Truro River

Truro in the
Middle Ages
A Conjectural Map

Newham

Chapter 2

From the Black Death
to the Reformation

In 1349 Ralph de Polwyl was installed as the new rector of St Mary's church, only four years after the previous incumbent had been appointed. This was at a time when plague was devastating the country, killing a third or more of the population, and the diocese of Exeter seems to have been badly affected. The Black Death is thought to have first arrived in Dorset the previous September, the germs being carried on merchant ships sailing from Bordeaux. From there it spread so rapidly that within a few weeks the Bishop of Exeter was ordering processions of supplication to be held throughout the diocese. By the early spring of 1349 reports of deaths started to be recorded in Cornwall. During that year there were 264 institutions to vacant livings in the see of Exeter,[1] including Kenwyn and St Clement, about twenty times the usual annual turnover, and some vacancies had to be left unfilled. On the nearby manor of Moresk nearly half of the holdings became vacant, so the evidence suggests that Truro and the area around it suffered badly. It was not only people who died: so too did animals. In many places bodies of sheep, oxen and other farm animals lay rotting in the fields, perhaps because of the plague, or some other disease that affected them, or from neglect because of the death or flight of their owners. Just over twelve years later the pestilence was back again with some severity and yet again St Mary's received a new rector, with John Dewy succeeding Ralph.

War with France, stopped only temporarily by the ravages of the Black Death, added to the problems, with the new Duke of Cornwall, Edward III's son Edward the Black Prince, expecting his Duchy to supply some of the necessary finance, and it was from the tin industry that much of his revenue came. A report highlighted the bad state of repair of Duchy property and it was as a result of this that the Duchy steward received orders in 1351 to build or buy a house in Truro for coinage.[2] In 1357 the Duke ordered four coinages a year, but this soon reverted to the usual two, probably because of the lack of tin as the industry suffered badly from the Black Death with loss of manpower. In the 1330s there had been some record coinages which peaked at over 700 tons, but in the early 1350s this dropped to less than 100 tons and was not to return to the higher levels until the last twenty years of the century.[3]

There is evidence that Truro's prosperity, dependent largely on trade and tin, slumped in the years following the Black Death not only because of the loss of people and the decline in the tin industry but also because of the war which lasted off and on from the late 1330s until 1453. Trade, both overseas and coastal, would have suffered as merchant ships were expected to help in the defence of the country as well as in carrying supplies to the armies in France. Orders were sent out in 1339 to all Cornishmen on the south coast to repel the French who were raiding. In 1351 there was an urgent demand for transport ships and in 1359, at the start of another campaign, Cornwall received orders for 300 sheaves of arrows and 1,000 bowstrings, which would all need transporting. This transportation of supplies and also of men may have been profitable for the individual ship owners but they also had to contend with the problem of piracy in the Channel, which became worse.

With the death of the Black Prince in 1376 and his father, Edward III, the following year, the main wars with France petered out for a time, but raids still continued. In 1377 Truro was attacked in spite of its relatively safe position at the head of the estuary; its storehouses were looted and ships in the port were stolen or sunk.[4] A disaster like this would destroy not only trade but confidence, which would take some time to restore. It is hardly surprising that Truro Burgesses protested against the taxes imposed on them. They sent a petition to Richard II asking for their payments to be reduced from over £12 to £2.10s, as houses were decayed and empty and the situation was so bad that people were thinking of forsaking their homes and moving elsewhere.[5] The Sheriff enquired into the situation and reported that the town was impoverished by pestilence and hostile invasion and was almost wholly wasted and uninhabited.[6]

This was not the only attack on the town because in 1404 there was another raid and this time it seems to have been even worse with the town set on fire.[7] A rental of the Bishop of Exeter, dated 1407-8, adds confirmation to the cumulative effects of the Black Death and the wars with evidence of vacant plots in the town being used as gardens.[8] In 1413 the Burgesses were again complaining about the taxes imposed and there was also a further problem which is still causing trouble in the town, flooding. Twenty-four years later, when Henry VI was desperate for money, a special tax was imposed on all foreigners. Each alien householder was charged 16d per annum for three years and all others were charged 6d for the same time. The list for Truro[9] recorded a number of such households, Scots, Irish, Breton, French and Dutch, with names like John Goldsmyth, Andrew Smyth and Wolf Maryner, indicating men concerned with metal work and ships. This perhaps illustrates the usual cosmopolitan mixture of the town or it might show that foreigners moved into the town during these difficult years.

The practical help and spiritual solace of the church could be especially important at such times and the rector of St Mary's was not always available. John Hamely was given three dispensations for leave of absence to study during his time as priest from 1328 to 1333, so would have seen little of his parishioners. Reginald Pridiaux, who followed him, was also given similar dispensations[10] and Thomas Wylle, who was rector from about 1370, had three-year periods of absence for study on two occasions.[11] It was perhaps at times like this that the presence of the Dominicans, the "Friars Preachers", was particularly welcome. Some of the friars were given the right to hear confessions, and one of them, Roger Tyrel, was specifically given this right in 1355 and again in 1371, for those people who spoke no English but only Cornish. The friars may have provided another sort of service: taking charge of the muniments of local people, as they did for at least one landed gentleman in later years, Peter Bevyll of Gwarnick in St Allen parish, who died in 1511. They frequently gave hospitality to clergymen travelling through Cornwall and it was they who entertained the Archbishop of Canterbury, William Courtenay, when he passed through Truro on his way to and from West Cornwall in 1384. In addition to this practical help the water from their well was reputed to have miraculous qualities for curing sore eyes.

Seal of the Friary, now in the Royal Cornwall Museum (Courtesy Roger Penhallurick)

The friary depended for its maintenance to a large extent on charitable bequests and over the years they received money not only from some of the bishops of Exeter, but also from knights, clerks and others. In the 1370s, for example, Bishop Grandisson left 40s, in 1417 John Meger, a pewterer, left 26s 8d for masses to be said for his soul, and in 1426 John Waryn, a clerk, left 10s.[12] The friary seems to have been expanding during the fourteenth century. In August 1354, when the Black Prince made his first visit to Cornwall, a high-profile stay at Restormel Castle, amongst the people who flocked there to see this famous young fighter, accompanied by the companions who had fought with him at Crecy, were some of the Truro Dominicans. There they received permission to take from his estate at Restormel ten oak trees suitable for beams to help them build their "new house". Twenty-one years later they extended their property by being granted a royal licence to purchase two pieces of land to enclose.

Truro was also in desperate need of financial help during these lean years and it was perhaps because of this that Pope Boniface IX gave an indulgence in 1400 to all who visited St Mary's church on 2 August each year. Indulgences were granted by the popes and bishops to repentant sinners to reduce the time of their punishment spent in purgatory. Usually these were partial indulgences for a limited period or a special occasion but sometimes a plenary indulgence, only granted by popes, might be given which would promise a full pardon for all the penance due. Unusually for a parish church this was the type of indulgence given to St Mary's church. The church was at least one hundred and fifty years old and the grant was perhaps an indication that major repairs or some rebuilding were needed and it would be an important source of money for this expensive work. This grant would be well advertised, perhaps by publicising it in church or fixing a notice to the church door, to ensure that as many people as possible would contribute.[13]

Pilgrims could be granted indulgences if they gave alms at a certain shrine or other holy place. Just outside Truro, near the top of Chapel Hill, St George's Chapel was licensed as newly-built in 1420. Like the leper house further down the hill, it was on the main routeway into the town from the west and was probably built to serve pilgrims and other travellers. In 1427 the Pope granted an indulgence of a hundred days to those pilgrims who gave alms for the conservation and repair of this chapel if they visited it during the time of the feast of St George, Whitsuntide and other important feast days. Eight years later the Bishop issued an indulgence of forty days for alms given for its repair.[14]

Bands of pilgrims riding or walking along the roads and trackways to visit shrines were a common sight in the Middle Ages. As Geoffrey Chaucer described in his Prologue to *The Canterbury Tales*, when spring came and travel became easier and the countryside was at its most appealing:

> *Thanne longen folk to goon on pilgrimages,*
> *And palmeres for to seken straunge strondes,*
> *To ferne halwes, kowthe in sondry londes.*

(Then people long to go on pilgrimage, and palmers to visit foreign shores, famous distant shrines in many lands. "Palmers" originally meant pilgrims who went to the Holy Land.) St Michael's Mount and the shrine of St Petroc at Bodmin were two of the main centres of pilgrimage in Cornwall, but the nearest one to Truro was the popular shrine of the Holy Trinity at St Day, remembered by many people in their wills, including two Truro men, the pewterer John Meger, and Thomas Tregian, a merchant. Truro people suffering from rheumatism would hope that prayers at this shrine would relieve their pain as it was reputed to cure the disease.[15] In the later sixteenth century, over forty years after it had been destroyed, John Norden wrote that "the resorte was so greate, as it made the people of the countye to bring all kinds of provision to that place, and so long it contynued with increase, that it grew to a kinde of market". Some pilgrims would want to go further afield to *seken straunge strondes*. One such pilgrimage set out from Truro in 1396 when William Rose of the *Seinte Marie* of Truro sailed with forty people for Spain, to visit one of Europe's greatest shrines, that of St James of Compostella.[16] Just as tourists today buy their holiday souvenirs, so those who went to Compostella would no doubt bring back the saint's memento, a cockle shell.

It was perhaps some Truro person who had travelled to Rome, either on pilgrimage or for trade, who founded the fraternity of the Blessed Mary of Portal. This is an unusual dedication in England, but there was an important shrine in Rome so named.[17] The chapel, which had a chaplain, warden and endowments, was built just outside the borough boundary on the east, probably near the bridge over the Allen. People left money for it in their wills, but little more is known about it. Its name has not been forgotten today because the Roman Catholic church in Truro has a similar dedication. Another religious guild, which may have had an aisle in St Mary's church, was also founded in the borough, dedicated to Jesus. Thomas Tregian, whose trading ship was also called the *Jesus*, left in 1517 the generous sum of twenty shillings and "one dole in Whelle (Wheal) Yest" to the "store of the gelde of Jhus here in Truru."[18]

Guilds like this were sometimes connected with particular occupations, and craft guilds developed in most towns during the fourteenth and fifteenth centuries. Members of trades, such as pewterers, tanners and weavers, combined to defend their own craft, the quality of their goods and the well-being of the members and their dependants. There are no records of such guilds in Truro, but the rules of the cobblers' guild of Helston from 1517 have survived and several are known to have operated in Bodmin, so we can assume that Truro also had its craft guilds. Richard Peauterer was recorded in the bishop's rental for 1407-8, and the making of pewter, with tin as one of its main raw materials, may well have been one of the skilled crafts protected by a guild in Truro.

The difficulties suffered by Truro during these years may have been the reason for the pewterer, John Meger, moving away from his home town to the greater attractions and opportunities of London (like many a person since). He represented Truro in Parliament and did not forget Truro people in his will when he died in 1419. He left money to some of his relations in the borough; to an honest chaplain at St Mary's church to pray for his soul and the souls of others; to Kenwyn church for vestments and ornaments in return for prayers for his soul; and to the friary for masses for his soul. A further 12d went to the shrine of St Day. He also remembered those less fortunate than himself, which would have been regarded as his Christian duty, because he left money to "every poor bed-lier" in Truro and Kenwyn, to blind people in the parish of St Kea and to the lepers on Chapel Hill.[19]

The fifteenth century continued to be a time of unrest, the wars against France flaring up again, followed by civil war with Yorkists and Lancastrians fighting for the crown, and then finally rebellions. This was made worse in Cornwall by rivalry between landed families eager for more power and status, which could lead to horrific violence, such as with the Courtenay and Bonville families over the stewardship of the Duchy of Cornwall and the Glynns and the Clemens over the deputy-stewardship. Truro men were directly concerned with at least one violent attack in 1426, when William Bodrugan, Lord of both Newham and Truro, who had inherited his manor from the Pridias family, was accused with others of violence in sorting out what seems to have been a family problem. The complaint was made by Robert Hull, William's step-grandfather who said that they broke into his house, assaulted and badly wounded him and then took away 20 horses, 100 oxen, 40 cows, 300 sheep and other goods. Amongst the Truro men involved were John Lercedekne of Truro, gent., Henry Rossaund of Truro, yeoman, John and Edward Nicholl of Truro, tanners, and others from Newham.[20]

William's son, Henry, also gained notoriety for piratical and other violent actions including breaking into the house of John Penpons in the borough of Truro.[21] On another occasion he attacked James Trefusis' house, broke into his ship, the *Bride* of Feock, and stole some of his property. He was close to Truro again when he attacked Polwhele Castle and threatened to burn it down.[22] The Polwhele family had occupied land north of Truro ever since 1140 when Matilda, William I's granddaughter, had rewarded her chamberlain, Drogo Polwheile, for his support in her cause. According to his eighteenth-century descendant, Richard Polwhele, this castle had "towered on a commanding site for ages", but when William of Worcester was visiting Otho of Polwhele, in 1473, he stated that the "castle" was reduced to ruins, probably by supporters of the Lancastrian cause, so perhaps Henry had carried out his threat before his support for the Yorkist cause had become firm.

During the fifteenth century the eastern half of Cornwall prospered much more than the western half where there was a slump in both the tin industry and agriculture. Truro and Lostwithiel were the two regular coinage towns, but Lostwithiel invariably dealt with more tin than Truro. Tin production declined to its lowest point in the early 1460s and there were long periods when Truro held no coinages at all, so one of the town's important sources of wealth was absent. With the reduction in tin output there was a corresponding reduction in demand for land. The revenue from Duchy mills in the west declined sharply during the fifteenth century, the one for the manor of Moresk, for example, falling from 7s in the early fourteenth century to only 2s in the late fifteenth, indicating that much less corn was being grown. The Duchy manors in the west of the county, such as Moresk, suffered from vacant and dilapidated holdings and falling rents,[23] and this poverty must have affected Truro markets. The relative wealth of the ports in the east of the county compared with those in the west is perhaps shown by the number of vessels impressed into the king's service in the last few years of the wars with France in the middle of the century. Fowey was by far the most important port supplying nineteen ships, while another sixteen came from Saltash, Landulph and Looe combined. Only twelve came from the west of the county, with Truro and Penryn both supplying just two each.[24]

It was in this poor western part of the county, at St Keverne, that trouble broke out in May 1497. Michael Joseph, the blacksmith (*an gof* in Cornish), fanned resentment against the tax imposed by the Tudor King, Henry VII, to send an army against the Scots who were supporting the claims to the English throne of the pretender Perkin Warbeck. How many Truro men joined the angry crowd when they marched through Truro on their way to Bodmin is not

The 500th anniversary of the 1497 Cornish Rebellion:
Truro people join the marchers from St Keverne

46

known. Certainly no Truro men of any standing seem to have become involved, but the news of the fighting at Blackheath and subsequent executions of the leaders did not deter Otis of Polwhele from joining Perkin Warbeck at Bodmin, after he arrived in Cornwall in early September to lead a second rebellion which ended in failure.[25] The fines imposed on the rebels must have been a heavy burden for many, but the economic situation was now slowly improving.

Tin output began to increase in the later years of the century as miners began digging into hillsides to extract ore in addition to the earlier method of tin streaming. Truro would benefit from this and the town was perhaps expanding as it recovered from its earlier decline. It was in the late fifteenth century that Middle Row was first recorded, a narrow row of houses stretching from the Coinage Hall to the bottom of what is now King Street, dividing modern Boscawen Street into two very narrow streets, so making full use of the flatter land close to the church, market and quays.[26]

A good indication that Truro was emerging from its economic depression is the success of one of its merchants, Thomas Tregian, whose wealth was based on tin and trade. He has been overshadowed by his more famous and tragic great-grandson, Francis, but it was he who built up the family fortunes. A.L.Rowse in *Tudor Cornwall* tells of one trading arrangement of his that was brought to court when he and another Truro man had failed to supply tin to a London merchant as promised, because the salt which he was to sell them had gone down in value and they refused to accept it. Rowse comments: "No doubt this was the way the great Tregian fortune was made."

By the early years of the sixteenth century Thomas was a very rich man. In those days the best investment was in land and in 1512 he was buying manors in various parts of Cornwall. Money and land brought status and his eldest son, John, moved in the highest circles, being an Esquire of the Body, Steward of the Chamber and Gentleman Sewer, to no less a person than the King himself, Henry VIII. In reward for his services John was granted by the King a life monopoly in the export of cowhides from Cornwall, which no doubt was very lucrative. He also married well, his second wife, Jane Wolvedon, coming from an ancient and wealthy family. This brought him the manor of Wolvedon, or Golden, not far from Probus, which became their home.[27]

Tregian wealth was created not just by sea-trading but also by more direct involvement in the tin industry. When Thomas made his will in 1517 John was already suitably provided for and so was remembered only by certain household items such as "my olde salte of sylver" and "the best bedde and the tabull in the hall." But to his son, Peers, went all Thomas' rights to the tin works at Poldice and "Whelle (Wheal) Yeste" on Killifreth Down, a half share in his blowing house where the tin was smelted, as well as 3,000 lbs of tin and a quarter share in his ship, the *Jesus*.[28] So Thomas had interests in the tin from its extraction to its smelting and then its transportation. In this way he was not unlike the more famous entrepreneurs of the eighteenth century, such as William Lemon and Thomas Daniell.

His will also included 40s to be left to the "Store of Our Lady of Truro". Another indication that in the early years of the sixteenth century Truro was beginning to prosper again was the almost complete rebuilding of the old parish church, and in one of the new windows the arms of Margaret Tregian, perhaps Thomas' wife, were emblazoned. This major undertaking began in 1504 when Sir John Arundell gave permission for the people of Truro to dig for stone at his manor of Truro Vean for the purpose of building "a churche and a newe towre", with "as many stonys as shall be nedefull and necessarye".[29] The south-east front of this new church, with its elaborate carvings, can still be appreciated today; it is incorporated into the Cathedral, and the oldest building that can now be seen in Truro. The original stones used for this aisle did not

The south-east front of St Mary's church.
Many of the facing stones are not original but were part of a major
facelift when the cathedral was being built in the 1880s.

come from Sir John's quarry but from the Pentewan quarry on the cliffs in St Austell Bay.[30] These would have been brought by boat to the town quay and then perhaps dragged on sledges or loaded onto ox-drawn carts to be taken through the narrow streets to the open space by the High Cross, ready for the skilled stone masons' chisels.

It can be difficult to visualise today in churches with bare stone or whitewashed walls the bright colours that once illuminated the walls and windows of medieval churches. One of the pillars in St Mary's aisle still has some traces of decoration, but nothing to show the terrors of Hell that sometimes loured from the walls, or images of St Christopher, the patron saint of travellers, and of Christ of the Trades, two of the favourite themes in Cornwall. These pictures, painted to instruct the people, were often on the north wall where they could

be seen by the parishioners as they entered the church, lit up by the windows on the south side. The glowing colours of the stained-glass of this period can best be admired today at St Neot church, on the edge of Bodmin Moor, where the stories of the Creation and of Saint Neot are displayed. In Truro a few pieces of original glass can still be seen in St Mary's aisle, but once the windows showed the badge and motto of the Dukes of Cornwall and the coats of arms of other important families, such as the Edgcumbes, Arundells and Bevilles, who had provided some of the necessary funds.[31] Sir Richard Edgcumbe of

Cotehele, one of Henry VII's most trusted ministers, had become the patron of the church when the King had granted him the manor of Newham and Truro which had been forfeited by Henry Bodrugan.

This ambitious new church with its elaborately-carved south and east fronts, large south porch, stained-glass windows and richly-carved waggon roof was probably undertaken in stages (as later with the Cathedral) depending on the supply of money. It was still unfinished in 1512 when Richard Trewyk of Truro died in London, where he was possibly on business, and left 10s "to the goods and works of the said church of Our Lady of Truro."[32] Another will, this time of a widow, Tomasine Bevyll, indicates that perhaps the south aisle was near completion by 1517 because she desired to be buried in the chancel of the "new ambulatory in our lady Church of Trurow". A date was inscribed on one of the windows, variously given as 1514, 1518, 1534 and 1544, with the second being the most likely, which may well be the date for the completion of this south aisle. Bodmin's new church had been erected in the previous century in only four years, but here the stonework was much plainer than on St Mary's church and Bodmin also had greater financial resources. Fourteen years to rebuild St Mary's is comparable to the rebuilding of the church of St Mary Magdalene in Launceston which was begun seven years later and is even more richly carved. Perhaps neither of these rebuilding projects was completed. Sir John Arundell had intended stone from his quarry to be used for a new tower in Truro but, as at St Mary Magdalene's, this was not erected, and the old tower may have remained. It might have been the original medieval one that was later described by Andrew Brice in the eighteenth century as "a pitiful little thing which contains a single bell looking rather like a pigeon-house than a church tower." Almost certainly the turmoil caused by the Reformation halted the building work.[33]

Henry VIII's quarrel with the pope in the 1530s brought revolutionary changes in the church which could arouse in people strong emotions. A sceptical attitude can be detected in the wording of a customs official's report of a pilgrimage that set out from Truro in 1537. In the spring of that year a Truro ship, the *Magdalen* with John Michell as captain, sailed for Brittany with a party of about fifty pilgrims aboard. The customs official scathingly described them as "a company of riotous persons feigning a pope-holy pilgrimage".[34] These pilgrims prevented him from searching the ship by knocking him over the side when he first tried to board. He did not give up but tried again near St Mawes and this time succeeded in boarding but was carried off unwillingly to France. They threatened to throw him overboard on a rope and tow him behind the stern, although they did not carry this out. In Brittany he spent a very uncomfortable three weeks before being rescued by men from another Cornish vessel. He came to no real harm, but this action against an official is perhaps an indication of the mood of the times.[35] In the north of England people had risen in rebellion against the dissolution of monasteries in 1536, but although there were mutterings in the St Keverne area at this time there was as yet no overt opposition.

The opportunity for such springtime and summer jaunts for pilgrimages in England was to become a thing of the past, as in 1538 shrines were ordered to be destroyed. In that same year Truro also lost its friary. In September royal officials arrived at the friary and there the prior and ten friars signed the "voluntary" surrender of their house to the King. "We the prior and convent of ye blacke fryers of truroye with one assent and consent without any maner of coaccyon or consell do gyve our house into ye handdes of ye lorde vysyter to ye kinges use."[36] The friars, who had ministered to the needs of people in Truro and its neighbourhood for about three hundred years, would now be expelled to make their own way in the world as best they could. Unlike the monks, the friars received no financial aid.

There was no indication that the friary had lost its appeal to local people. In the immediate years leading up to this dissolution they were still remembering it in their wills. Thomas Tregian had left forty shillings in 1517, and Thomas Killigrew and John Cavell both left money for masses to be said for their souls. Some requested burial in their church as did John Hariwell in 1515 who added, "I wyll that upon my grave be sett a marble stone". In 1528 Thomas Tretherffe of Ladock had left 10s to the friars to sing a "solemn dirge and mass of requiem" for his soul.[37] What Truro people felt about this dissolution is not recorded. The Mayor and other town officials were present when an inventory was drawn up and they received the furnishings for safekeeping, which were not very valuable, while the Visitor took away sixteen score ounces of broken silver and plate after all debts had been paid. No doubt the stone of the chapel and other buildings was used elsewhere and hardly any of this now remains. The Royal Cornwall Museum has one of its limestone capitals displayed on the wall, and it is just possible that the archway in the grounds of the soon-to-be-closed City Hospital came from stones of the friary.[38] The seal of the friary can also be seen in the museum, discovered 300 years later, in 1842, in the garden of a house near Canterbury.

When John Leland visited Truro soon afterwards he referred to the friary that had once been there "on the West Arme (of the creek) yn Kenwyn streate".

He also mentioned the site of the castle, "now clene doun". The castle had been dismantled many years before, but the circular mound was being used, as Leland stated, as "a shoting and playing Place." No doubt butts were set up here for archery practice, Cornish longbowmen being renowned, perhaps wrestling matches were also held here, but the reference to "playing place" shows that this was probably also being used as Truro's "plain-an-gwarry", where miracle plays would be performed on holy days and feast days, the raised sides providing standing space for the audience and the flat, central part an acting area for the players. *The Life of St Meriasek*, the story of Camborne's saint, was completed in the Cornish language, probably by a canon of Glasney, in 1504, and others from this centre of Cornish literature probably wrote the earlier *Ordinalia*, again in Cornish, a cycle of three plays on the Creation, the Passion and the Resurrection, which would need three days to perform.[39] Plays like these, written in Cornish for a mass audience, would have entertained Truro people.

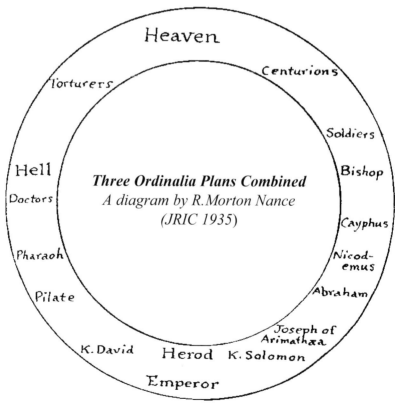

Three Ordinalia Plans Combined
A diagram by R.Morton Nance
(JRIC 1935)

From the Black Death to the Reformation

The arrangements of the playing place were carefully thought through, based on the design of churches where they were originally performed. On the east side, the altar end of the church, was the place for Heaven, in Truro looking out over the Allen river towards St Clement. Opposite would be the area for important worldly powers, such as kings and emperors. The south, the priest's door side, looking out over the town, was the place for the clergymen and "good" characters, while on the north was hell, the side for the devil and other "bad" characters. There was plenty of opportunity for instruction of the people, with the good characters getting their reward in heaven and the bad going to the everlasting torments of hell. There were opportunities for exciting fights, music and dancing, bawdy humour, and local references to hold the interest of the audience, and no doubt special effects for the fires of hell and sudden miraculous appearances.[40]

The Reformation meant that plays like these would soon be out of fashion, as would the Cornish language, especially with the introduction of the New English Prayer Book in 1549, which provoked yet another rebellion by Cornish men, this time joined by Devonians. Other changes affecting people's religious practices probably fuelled the ill-feeling over the Prayer Book. In 1548 the religious guilds, which may have been responsible for performances of some of the miracle plays, were abolished so Truro people lost the guilds of St Nicholas, the Blessed Mary of Portal and Jesus. At the same time chantries were dissolved. The founding of chantries, where priests could pray for the souls of the departed, had been popular in the late Middle Ages. Their dissolution could upset many people who would now lose this personal link with their ancestors whose money had enriched these chapels. St Mary's church had a chantry founded by the Langharne or Lagherne family of Tregavethan whose endowment provided for a priest to pray for the souls of the founder and his family.[41] However, a Chantry Certificate of 1549 shows that Stephen Langharne had already taken the income for himself, perhaps anticipating the confiscations to come.

The foundation of Truro Grammar School, which lasted for over four hundred years, seems to have emerged from the dissolution of the Langharne Chantry. Until the sixteenth century education, such as it was, had been the responsibility of churchmen, often monks or chantry priests. When the chantries were dissolved income from them was sometimes used for providing schools, and this seems to have happened in Truro. A Chantry Certificate of 1547 has this entry: "Chantry - A Stipendiary of the benevolence of the Mayor and Burgesses to Minister in the Church and keep a Schole." Another certificate of

Duntv.E.&Pub.Nid.by.Twigs, Oristin from a Sketch by W.Twigy.

The south porch, from an engraving, courtesy RIC

1550 mentioned "Richard Fosse, priest, incumbent and schoolmaster there, at the age of 50 years hath for his salary £6 13s 4d."[42] Education might still be in the hands of clergymen, but the important men of the borough were also now involved in this school, where the sons of the Burgesses, the chief merchants and artisans, could be educated. Little is known about its earliest years, but it has been suggested that the large south porch of St Mary's church may well have acted as a schoolroom. When separate premises were later provided for the school, they were situated very close to the church in St Mary's Street.

The more influential people of Truro must have accepted these momentous changes. None seems to have been involved in the Prayer Book Rebellion of 1549 so Truro did not suffer, as did the Mayor of Bodmin and the Portreeve of St Ives, from the gallows humour of Anthony Kingston who was sent to deal with the aftermath. Truro's losses were not as great as Bodmin's, and the borough was once again enjoying the prosperity brought by the twice-yearly coinages. When Queen Mary tried to turn the church in England back to the control of Rome, John Melhuish, a merchant who represented Truro in Parliament, strongly opposed her attempts. He with five other Cornish MPs were amongst the thirty seven members who took the extreme step of walking out of the House of Commons as a protest.[43] The queen could not ignore this. The Attorney General indicted them, but Mary died before they could be brought to trial, and religious policy changed yet again with the accession of her sister Elizabeth.

References

[1] Elliott-Binns, 1955
[2] Pennington, 1973
[3] Hatcher, 1970
[4] Pearse, 1963
[5] Jennings, P., "The Expansion of Truro," JRIC Volume XV
[6] Douch, 1977
[7] Pearse, 1963
[8] Personal communication, Dr Joanna Mattingly
[9] Henderson, C., transcription held by RIC
[10] Bishop Grandison's Register
[11] Bullock, 1948
[12] Henderson, C., JRIC, 1958
[13] Orme, N., "Indulgences in Medieval Cornwall", JRIC, 1992
[14] Henderson, C., JRIC, 1958
[15] Annear, Paul, *The Church and Chapel of the Holy Trinity, St Day*, Author, 1994
[16] Halliday, 1959
[17] Douch, 1977
[18] Taylor, the Rev. T.B., "Francis Tregian, his Family and Possessions", JRIC, 1910
[19] Jennings, P., JRIC XIII; Annear, Paul, op. cit., 1994; also personal communication on WEA course
[20] Whetter, J., "William Bodrugan, Soldier and Knight", Old Cornwall, Spring 1990
[21] Payton, 1996
[22] Rowse, 1941
[23] Hatcher, 1970
[24] Halliday, 1959
[25] Rowse, 1941
[26] Truro Buildings Research Group, *Boscawen Street Area*, University of Exeter, n.d.
[27] Boyan & Lamb, 1948
[28] Taylor, the Rev. T.B., op. cit., JRIC, 1910
[29] Spry, W., "The Dominican Friary and St Mary's Church", Report of the RIC, 1840

[30] Cartwright, A., *Truro Cathedral Rock Trail* (leaflet)
[31] Spry, W., op. cit, 1840
[32] Henderson, C., Ecclesiastical Antiquities, JRIC, 1960
[33] Bullock, 1948
[34] Pounds, N., "Ports and Shipping of the Fal", JRIC, 1946
[35] Rowse, 1941
[36] Whitley, H.M., "Inventories of the Cornish Friaries", JRIC VIII
[37] Henderson, C., Ecclesiastical Antiquities, JRIC, 1958
[38] Personal communication on WEA course
[39] Whetter, J., *The History of Glasney College*, Tabb House, 1988
[40] Nance, R.Morton, "The Plen an gwary or Cornish Playing Place", JRIC, 1935
[41] Davidson, 1970
[42] ibid.
[43] Jennings, P., "The Parliamentary History of Truro 1469-1660", JRIC XIV

Chapter 3

Traders, Tin and Pirates

An Act of Parliament was passed in 1540 to repair some of the decayed towns of Cornwall, including Truro. Although no action was taken, the security of the port and town was improved by the building of castles to defend the haven of the Fal. The vulnerability of the Fal estuary had been shown all too clearly in January 1537 when a Spanish fleet anchored in Carrick Roads. This was not unusual as it was a harbour of refuge from storms for ships sailing to and from the west coast of England and the ports of the continent. What was unusual was that four French warships arrived soon afterwards and the Spaniards, perhaps fearing for their cargo, began shooting at them and for three hours "great gunshot passed between them." The French, chased by the Spanish ships, were driven up the river almost as far as Truro where they went aground near Malpas. Sir John Arundell went out to the Spanish ships and told them to stop or he would "raise the county upon them." When he reported this incident to Henry VIII's minister, Thomas Cromwell, he ended: "I and all the county will desire the King's Grace that we may have blockhouses made upon our haven."[1]

Malpas, from a 19th-century engraving,
courtesy Cornish Studies Library, Redruth

Traders, Tin and Pirates

It would take more than this one incident to justify the expenses involved but, in spite of enmity between France and Spain, there was a real fear that they might combine in an attack on England because of Henry's break with the Pope, and a survey of the coasts showed how unprotected Cornwall was. Carrick Roads with its deep-water haven would have been ideal to shelter an enemy fleet which could bring supplies to an invading army.[2] The plans for St Mawes and Pendennis were probably both prepared in 1542 when defences along the south coast generally, not just in Cornwall, were being strengthened, partly financed by Henry's acquisition of the monasteries, and soon the castles were completed, one on each side of the mouth of the Fal.

Pendennis Castle

The tin trade from Truro was now increasing rapidly as the centre of the tin industry was moving westwards and the coinage here was becoming more important than that of Lostwithiel. In 1305 84% of all the tin produced in Cornwall had come from the eastern part of the county with Bodmin and Lostwithiel as the main coinage towns. But by the second half of the sixteenth century the position had changed radically. In 1577 nearly three times as much tin was coined in Truro as in Lostwithiel, with Helston coining almost as much. These two towns gained even more over the next thirty years.[3]

Most tin was still being produced by open works or streaming, but the sixteenth century also saw the development of underground mining. One of the landowning families who fully exploited their tin resources were the

Godolphins. "No greater Tynne Workes yn al Cornwal then be on Sir William Godolcan's Ground," wrote John Leland from his observations, when he journeyed from Marazion to Helston. Sir William Godolphin's son, another William, was rewarded with the position of Comptroller of the Stannaries by Henry VIII after he had used Cornish miners in 1544 to undermine the walls of Boulogne, which Henry was besieging. This appointment caused problems in Truro when Henry VIII's daughter, Mary, appointed William Isham to this position.

On 4 July 1554 when coinage was about to begin, a large group of men "came in riotous manner in Trurowe with swordes and dagers." At the closed door of the Coinage Hall there was an argument, and when the door was opened they rushed in with weapons drawn and "with very spytefulle and crewelle woordes" ordered William Isham in the name of Sir William Godolphin to leave and "no further meddle with the said offyce." Isham was not to be intimidated and demanded the coinage hammer from one of the men who had snatched it up and was carrying it on his shoulder. The man refused and when Isham tried to grab it the man drew his dagger and might have wounded or killed him if one of the porters had not rushed forward and stopped him. Isham was then dragged to the door, at which point he shouted for someone to fetch the Mayor to keep the peace. The Mayor, however, refused to become involved in a matter which he said did not concern him. This matter was later brought before the Court of the Star Chamber but the records do not show how it was settled.[4]

Among the important merchant families of Truro at this time were the Michells, a name that occurs in Truro from the Middle Ages right up to the twentieth century, often of merchants and traders. In 1440 John Michell had been one of the wardens for the Fraternity of the Blessed Mary of Portal. Another John was recorded in a tax return of Henry VIII's reign as one of the richest men in the borough and it was probably he or his son who had captained the *Magdalen* on its "pope-holy" pilgrimage in 1537. During Queen Elizabeth's reign John Michell, who was MP for Truro 1562-3, was having problems with pirates. The attack suffered by one of his ships in 1568 would not have happened if the castles at Pendennis and St Mawes had been kept in a good state of readiness, but a survey in 1574 showed that the Fal coastal defences had deteriorated so badly that they were in an almost unusable state. This may have suited the Killigrews of Arwenack at the mouth of the Fal, who were gaining a notorious reputation for their piratical exploits, but they were not the only ones, and of course there were complaints from Cornish shipowners of similar actions against their vessels. In 1568 John Michell reported that his ship, the *George*, with a cargo of wine worth £800, was taken by French pirates from its anchorage within sight of the town and sailed back to Brittany. The pirates made a very good haul on this occasion as they took two other English ships and two Flemish ones. They stripped the *George*, not only of its cargo but also of the armaments and other fitments and it was then wrecked on the rocks. He complained that this was his third ship to be taken by French pirates in seven years and reckoned that he had lost £3,000 and had had no recompense.[5]

Two years later the Vice Admiral of Cornwall received a letter from Queen Elizabeth's Privy Council about complaints from two Breton merchants, backed up by the French ambassador, against John Michell for taking their ship with its cargo. They wanted their goods returned or to be compensated for the loss. A month later, presumably with nothing settled over this, John was being ordered to appear before the lords of the Privy Council "to answer unto his doings...as he will answer for the country at his peril."[6] Was this capture of a Breton ship by John Michell his way of taking direct action to gain compensation for his earlier loss or was it all more complex than this? The answers are frustratingly missing, nor do we know how he responded to the order of the Privy Council or what the outcome was for him. Politically it was a bad time to annoy the French, as delicate negotiations were under way for a possible marriage between Queen Elizabeth and the French king's brother. So the queen's council may have treated this case seriously or just given the appearance of doing so for the benefit of the French ambassador.

Foreign policy with France and Spain and fears over the possible resurgence of Roman Catholicism were intimately connected during these years as Truro people were to witness. In June 1577 the Sheriff of Cornwall, Sir Richard Grenville, rode into town with soldiers escorting a small band of prisoners. Chief amongst these were Francis Tregian of Golden Manor, the great-grandson of the wealthy Truro merchant Thomas Tregian, and the man who acted as his steward, Cuthbert Mayne. Cuthbert was in fact a Roman Catholic priest who had been trained at Douai and was secretly ministering to the spiritual needs of the Catholic community in Cornwall, at a time when to be a declared Catholic was tantamount to being a traitor in the eyes of many.

The bishop was in Truro on a visitation partly because of the fear of the influence of Catholic recusants (those who refused to attend the services of the Anglican church). He examined the men, ridicule being used as one method to try and change their beliefs. Francis was treated "as a man bereft of his wits," but there was no change of heart so examples had to be made of them.[7] Francis Tregian was imprisoned for many years in London before finally being allowed to live in exile in Portugal, but a worse fate befell the priest. On 29 November 1577 Cuthbert Mayne was hanged on a high gallows in Launceston on market day, the first Catholic martyr of Elizabeth's reign. Truro must have been considered safe from Catholic influences as it was Tregony, Bodmin, Wadebridge and Barnstaple in Devon, the nearest town to his childhood home, which were all sent a portion of his body to display as a warning to others.

The power and influence that Thomas Tregian had helped to engineer for his eldest son were now lost by his descendants. All the lands of the Tregian inheritance were divided up amongst others greedy for the spoils. Francis' wife, Mary (Arundell), heavily pregnant, was turned out of their splendid new house at Golden at dead of night with three of her young children. With borrowed horses she made her way to London, stopping only to give birth to her second daughter, and then did all she could to help her husband.[8]

This cruel treatment has to be seen against the growing fear of neighbouring Catholic countries. A few years earlier, in 1572, French Catholics had turned on French Protestants in the bloody Massacre of St Bartholomew's Eve, and Francis Drake and other sailors had returned from the New World with stories of Spanish treachery against English ships and men. France was only a few miles away across the Channel, and Spain was also too close for comfort with its armies in the Netherlands fighting Dutch Protestants and disrupting the important English cloth trade in that area. Enmity between England and Spain became worse after Francis Drake's circumnavigation of the world in 1577-80, sailing unharmed through Spanish waters in the New World and attacking their ships. John Michell's son, Peter, was one of nine young gentlemen who sailed with him on this momentous voyage,[9] so Truro people would have had a first-hand account of the fights won, the strange lands seen and the Spanish treasures stolen. It was in this atmosphere of mistrust that war finally broke out between England and Spain, which led to the Spanish Armada of 1588.

Cornish ships and men were quickly gathered together for defence of the coasts, some joining Drake at Plymouth, and 3,000 or more men were mustered in Cornwall for the militia, under the command of Sir Richard Grenville, to fight off the enemy if they tried to land. The sighting of this huge fleet off the Lizard, the hasty preparations, the fear of a Spanish landing in the Fal, the news of the first engagement off Looe, all must have caused worry and upset in Truro. The relief must have been great when those massed sails disappeared

61

over the horizon, followed some time later by the news that strong winds had scattered the fleet.

It must have been in a euphoric mood that Truro received a new charter from the Queen in 1589. Even though no action had followed Henry VIII's Act for the repair of decayed Cornish towns, by the 1580s Truro was well-kept and prosperous. John Nordern described it as "a pretty compacted town, well-peopled and wealthy merchants; for although it be remote from the haven yet it exceedeth Penryn, the haven-town for providence, traffic and good government. It is one of the towns privileged for the coinage of tin. …There is not a town in the west part of the shire more commendable for neatness of buildings and for being served of all kinds of necessaries." He then added, "Nor more discommendable for pride of the people." No doubt the "proud" Burgesses celebrated their new charter with feasting, perhaps accompanied by the music of young Giles Farnaby, who was probably born in the town twenty five years earlier and was to become well-known in London for his madrigals and keyboard music.

The new charter declared that the Borough of Truro "from henceforth shall be a Free Borough and that the said inhabitants...from henceforth for ever may and shall be one Corporate and Body Politic..." It gave Truro a Mayor and twenty-four Capital Burgesses who would elect four Aldermen from amongst their ranks "out of the better and most honest sort" to help the Mayor, and these Burgesses would also have the right to elect Truro's two Members of Parliament. Elections for the Mayor and Aldermen were to be held once a year in early October. Having a Mayor was not new for the borough: reference had been made to this office in the fifteenth century; but the borough council was now put on a more regular footing. It had the power to nominate "one honest and fit person to be a Recorder of the said Borough" and also to elect a steward of the court, and two serjeants at mace, as well as a coroner from "amongst the honester Burgesses."

No-one was able to sell goods in the borough or to open up a shop without the consent of the council, with exception given during the time of fairs, and to butchers and victuallers. The Mayor was to act as the clerk of the market and two market days could now be held every week, on Saturdays as before and now also on Wednesdays if it did not adversely affect other nearby towns. Three fairs could be held annually: on the Wednesday before Easter, the Wednesday of Whitsun week and 8 December.

The charter emphasised that Truro was "the principal place where the tin hath been and is usually coined and from thence transported to other parts,

*The two serjeants at mace escorting the Mayor and
Mayoress of Truro in the March for Cornwall, May 1997*

by reason wherof a certain annual custom of at least one thousand marks has
been heretofore yearly paid." It also indicated a problem that bedevils Truro
as a port to the present day: the silting up of the river because of the wastes
from mining brought down by the streams. "Ships of 100 tons well laden
could and were accustomed to come into the said port, but now ships of 30
tons are scarcely able to enter the said port." The charter stressed that
"inhabitants of the same Borough do endeavour by all means to preserve the
Port by continual cleansing and repairing of the said Port there, that ships
coming there might have their accustomed course, even unto the quay of the
said Borough." In spite of these problems Truro was still the main port on the
Fal.

The charter named the men that Elizabeth wanted on this council with
the aptly named Thomas Burgess as the first Mayor. Another Burgess, John,
was named as a Capital Burgess and two other families were also prominent,
Mi(t)chell and Robarts. John Michell was named as the steward and his brother
Hugh as one of the Capital Burgesses. A monument in St Mary's was erected
in the early seventeenth century in memory of three Mi(t)chell brothers. Hals,
the early eighteenth century historian, who cannot always be relied on, recalled

that it was in memory of Thomas, John and James with the words: "One God, one womb, one tomb."[10]   However, it is possible that the names are not completely correct as there were at least seven Michell brothers, including Peter who had sailed with Drake. The second-eldest, James, who was a very wealthy man with influential friends from the county families such as Francis Godolphin, Francis Basset, Hugh Boscawen and John Trefusis, left in 1628 the large sum of £100 "for a tomb to be made and laid for and upon the corpses of myself and my said brother Hugh."[11]

John, Richard and William Roberts or Robarts were also included as Burgesses. The Robarts (later spelt Robartes) were another merchant family who played an important part in Truro's history, gained wealth and, like the Tregians, put much of it into land and status.   A grand and colourful monument, (photographed below) can be seen in the cathedral to the John Robarts mentioned in the charter, who died in 1614.   He is described there as "grave, honest and very discreet", important attributes for a merchant and money-lender.

His father, Richard, might have been a servant of the Godolphins (whose tin works had so impressed John Leland) before he moved to Truro, where he cornered the market in timber, storing a huge supply in the town.[12]   This commodity was in short supply but in great demand for many purposes especially for charcoal for tin smelting. Richard made contracts not only with owners of coppices but also those with furze downs and peat bottoms and brought in coal from South Wales, so in this way he began to build up the

64

prosperity of his family.[13]

John, his son, made a good marriage into the influential family of Gavrigan, and continued not only to trade successfully in timber and tin, but also to use some of his wealth lending out money to mine adventurers (shareholders), with his debtors paying him in tin. (More capital was now necessary with the increase in underground mining.) During the last part of the sixteenth century tin production rose with Truro and Helston benefiting as the main coinage towns. In 1595 at the Michaelmas coinage 136,000 lbs of tin were coined in Truro, more than at any of the other four coinage towns, and Truro and Helston together coined over five times the amount dealt with in Lostwithiel and Liskeard.[14] It might have been the London tin farmers who gained most from this trade,[15] but the Robartes also benefited from this increase in tin production and John's estate grew to be worth many thousands of pounds.

This wealth was displayed in the Robartes' Great House, in the centre of the town. Its frontage, on what is now Boscawen Street, was quite narrow, but it stretched back towards High Cross beside and over where Pearsons Ope is today. It was "great" in two senses: it was taller than usual, three main storeys with attics, and with dimensions larger than other merchants' houses known in Cornwall at that time.[16] Stone fireplaces, mullioned windows, spacious rooms, one at least with an elaborately carved doorway, all proclaimed great wealth. (The door jambs, which may date from the middle of the seventeenth century, were saved from destruction by Mr Douch, curator of the County Museum, when the last remnants of this fine house were demolished in 1960. This destruction was to make way for the expansion of the Midland Bank. Perhaps John Robarts, money lender, would have approved, but it was possibly a sad loss for the town.)

This was not the only fine house that this influential family was to own. John's son, another Richard, knighted in 1616 and ennobled in 1625, bought in 1620 the large estate of Lanhydrock near Bodmin, once the property of the priory there and today belonging to the National Trust. He began the building of his country mansion, which was completed after his death by his son, another John, but the Great House possibly remained their town house until later in the century.

When Richard Carew's *Survey of Cornwall* was published at the beginning of the seventeenth century, when the Great House would have been newly-built, he described Truro "as the principal town of the haven privileged with a mayoralty, and benefited with the general western sessions, coinages, markets, fairs &c. ...I hold it to have got the start in wealth of any other Cornish town, and to come behind none in buildings, Launceston only excepted, where there is more use and profit of fair lodgings through the county assizes." He then added this criticism: "I wish that they would likewise deserve praise for getting and employing their riches in some industrious trade to the good of their country, as the harbour's opportunity inviteth them."

This seems a rather harsh criticism for a town that had prosperous merchants as well as many other people involved in making and selling goods. One family making its mark at this time were the Daniells (or Daniels), a large Kenwyn family. The five eldest sons of Alexander and Agnes Daniell were provided for by their father with land, but there was was not enough for the two youngest ones, Jenkin (or Jenken) and Richard, so some other means of livelihood had to be found for them. Jenkin was apprenticed to a local merchant and in due course became a merchant and draper in Truro. Richard was sent in 1579 to a merchant in London. Eight years later, a year before the threat of the Spanish Armada, he was made a Freeman of the Drapers' Company and a Freeman of the City of London. He had been in the Low Countries earlier for his master and in 1590 he returned there, married a wealthy widow, went into partnership with two London merchants and prospered. He finally returned to live in Truro in 1614, having already sent his son Alexander back home for his schooling and bought land in Pydar Street for building a new house.[17]

IEN
KEN
DAN
IEL
MA
IOR.

T.   B.
WHO SEKS TO FIND
ETERNAL TREASVRE
MVST VSE NO GVILE
IN WAIGHT OR MEA
SVRE * 1615.

In October of that same year Jenkin was made Mayor. His name was recorded in stone on the market house and town hall which was built at this time, with the council chamber supported on sturdy pillars above an open-sided market hall at the end of what is now King Street. His carved homily to encourage honesty in the market traders was not destroyed when this market hall was pulled down in the early years of the nineteenth century, but it was taken to both the new market hall in Boscawen Street and then its successor of the mid-

nineteenth century, the one whose Italianate façade still graces the main street.
When Jenkin died a few years later the inventory for his shop, which may have been close to the market house against the west wall of the Robartes Great House, showed that besides supplying high class drapery goods, such as "cobweb lawn", "lyons rash", black silk lace and taffeta from the eastern Mediterranean, he also catered for a much wider demand. His stock showed as great a variety as a large department store today, including French girdles, school text books, dice, glasses, red sealing wax, timber shovels, muskets, pikes, swords, candy and salt.[18] How this multifarious collection was fitted into small premises is difficult to imagine.

Jenkin may have made it to the top of Truro society, but his fortune was no match for his younger brother's. In fact Richard was extremely generous to Jenkin, lending him large amounts of money that were never fully repaid. He was still owed over £560 at the time of Jenkin's death which his son, Jacob, promised his dying father that he would repay but never did. Richard was also elected a Capital Burgess becoming Mayor in 1622 and then went on to represent Truro in Parliament in 1624 and 1628.[19]

A contemporary of Jenkin's, whose name has also survived inscribed on stone (although now difficult to read), was Henry Williams. He was also a draper and woollen merchant who, like others at this time, made a considerable fortune from this trade. Perhaps it was his extreme thoughtfulness for other people, shown in his generosity, which led some people close to Henry to denounce him as a lunatic. Most unusually he made a liberal gift of land to the borough council in 1623 to improve its finances, and by his will he provided almshouses (shown on the left as they used to be) for ten poor people, endowing them with considerable property in and around Truro. These almshouses, opened in 1631 on Pydar Street where the Carrick District Council Offices now stand, included a meadow for the inmates to keep a cow. The inscribed stones, originally above the gateway leading into the courtyard around which the almshouses were built, can now be seen on the other side of the road in the garden of new bungalows built to replace them in 1970. (See photograph below.) When this likeable man died in 1629 he also gave £40 to provide one penny or a pennyworth of bread to twelve of the poorest people every Sunday "besides the poore of my Hospital", and £100 to enable ten poor craftsmen to take on poor children as apprentices."[20]

In these early years of the seventeenth century, but especially during the 1620s, Cornish ports and ships were under constant threat from pirates, some from across the Channel operating mainly from Dunkirk, then part of the Spanish Netherlands, but the most notorious ones were the Barbary pirates. These "Turks" as they were called operated from ports on the north coast of Africa, the Barbary coast, and captured many trading vessels sailing in the waters of the Bay of Biscay and around Spain and Portugal to the Mediterranean, but they also began to prey on shipping close to the coasts of Cornwall. Many Cornish ships were taken, the men becoming slaves if not killed in the fighting. Records from Cornish parishes show money being given for ransoming prisoners or for helping those who had suffered.[21]

A slate monument to Owen Phippen, or Fitzpen, still exists in the cathedral, erected after his death in 1636 by his brother, George, the schoolmaster and rector of St Mary's. Owen "who travelled over many parts of the world" was captured by Turkish pirates in 1620. He was obviously a leader and a man of spirit who was not prepared to die in slavery on a pirate's ship, because a few years later he led ten other captives to fight for their freedom. After a three hour fight with six of their number being killed, they got control of the pirate ship and Owen, as captain, sailed it safely into a Spanish port. He then sold his prize for £6,000 and returned home to Cornwall. If this is all true he profited financially from his ordeal, but for most people a pirate raid was not only frightening, it could be disastrous.

1625 was an especially bad year with pirates threatening all the coasts of Cornwall and fishermen and traders afraid to put to sea, creating shortages of food, especially fish, and other essential items. Looe on the south coast was particularly badly affected losing eighty mariners in ten days, and rumour was rife. Lundy off the north coast was reported to have been taken, and sixty men, women and children were said to have been captured in church in Mount's Bay and carried off as slaves. There is no evidence for this[22] but the fact that people were ready to believe the stories shows how scared they were. The following year the deputy-governor of Pendennis Castle was reporting Turks and Dunkirkers lurking in the area and feared they were planning to capture the Isles of Scilly. He requested more protection for the haven of the Fal as the defences of both castles were again badly maintained, but this fell on deaf ears.

The situation was not helped by war. In 1624 England was at war with Spain and then three years later with France as well. In 1626 there was a threat of Spanish attacks and a muster was called at Bodmin to which Truro Burgesses refused to send their trained bands, excusing their action because of the need to defend the valuable tin stocks in the town.[23] Eighty large ships had been spotted off the south coast, thought to be a Spanish invasion fleet, so Truro must have felt especially vulnerable. The Mayor of Penryn sent an urgent message to his counterpart in Truro, who sent it on to St Austell and so eventually the news reached the king's council in London. Luckily nothing came of this threat, which was just as well as the governor of Pendennis Castle was complaining early the following year that soldiers had died from malnutrition because the king's council had sent no supplies or money for their pay. This particular situation was remedied but the threat from pirates still continued into the next decade. In 1640 traders and fishermen feared for their lives and the safety of their boats and cargoes as a fleet of sixty Turkish ships was reported lying in wait off the Lizard.[24]

Truro's trade must have been affected by these alarms, but Truro itself was safer than those towns and villages right on the coast and for most people life must have carried on much as normal. The tanners and dyers were carrying on their everyday tasks in their premises on the western side of Pydar Street, where they could make use of the running water of the mill leat at the back of their properties.[25] The name "Tanyard Court", off Pydar Street, is a reminder of this once important industry. At the upper end of the street, where the town gave way to the country, the open field of Gweal Castel was being enclosed, turning the strips or stitches of land into long, hedged fields; the medieval idea of community farming was now ending. However, townspeople still had land and animals: for example Humphrey Soper, a prosperous tanner, kept four cows, twelve pigs and a horse, and Jenkin Daniell had three horses and a pig.[26]

The farmers still came in to sell their produce in the weekly or twice-weekly market. Cattle and other farm animals were sold around the High Cross area and from there market stalls stretched along the widest street in the town (now King Street) down to the Market House where the butchers sold their meat. This congested area around the Market House, Middle Row and St Nicholas Street was where most of the shops were found, such as the cobblers, saddlers, drapers and coopers.[27]

It was probably in this area that Gregory Angilly had his shop, stocked at the time of his death in 1626 with a huge variety of goods. These included haberdashery such as stitching silk, buttons and garters, but also many other items, for example 28 dozen playing cards, gunpowder, a dozen horn books and a large quantity of tobacco with a box of clay pipes, showing that even at this early date imports from the New World were already changing people's habits.[28]

At the east end of Middle Row, opposite the Coinage Hall, was a small prison with what was described as a dungeon on the ground floor. Stocks were set up outside for the punishment of some miscreants, and anyone found guilty of theft was liable to be flogged from the prison right round Middle Row. Almost opposite this prison, on the north side of what is now Boscawen Street, seems to have been a tennis court, an enclosed area for "royal" tennis.[29] Perhaps the younger members of the Michell, Daniell and Roberts families met here with their friends to test their skills in this energetic game.

On the south side was the prestigious inn, the Bull, close to the site of the present City Hall, ideally placed to accommodate visitors during the times of coinage. Along this side also were the houses of some of the wealthier merchants with their properties stretching to the banks of the River Kenwyn where boats could be moored. A recent archaeological survey during the reconstruction of the City Hall[30] has found evidence of infilling on the mudflats of the river so some reclamation might have started at this time with the growing need for more land. On the quays was all the bustle of the port. Here the tin ingots were loaded after coinage on to vessels bound for London. Here too slate, cloth and corn were taken from warehouses to the ships sailing to Ireland, Spain or France. Ships arrived with timber from Ireland and coal from South Wales, while from France and Spain came more exotic goods such as wine, spirits, fruit[31] and no doubt some of the high-class materials that Jenkin Daniell bought in for his shop.

The wealthier families of the town did not have to depend on imports for all their sophisticated possessions. Truro probably had pewterers using the locally produced tin for making tableware, and the town also had at least one goldsmith, John Parnell. He had a large property where today Lemon Street joins Boscawen Street stretching back to the river. The term goldsmith also includes working in silver, and only a mile or so from the town centre the Polwhele lead and silver mine was perhaps already producing the necessary raw material for his fine work. It was possibly he who crafted the two silver maces still carried by the serjeants at arms attending the Mayor on official occasions. It was almost certainly in these premises that a royal mint to manufacture money was established in 1642.[32] The reason for this was the outbreak of civil war.

References

[1] Whitley, H.M., "Cornwall and the Spanish Armada", JRIC VIII
[2] Johns,1992
[3] Maclean, J., "The Tin Trade of Cornwall in the Reigns of Elizabeth and James", RIC IV
[4] Henderson, Calendar No. 3
[5] Whitley, H.M., JRIC VIII
[6] Jennings, P., Researches
[7] Boyan and Lamb, 1955
[8] ibid.
[9] Michell, D., *The Ancient Family of Michell*, Carminow House, 1994
[10] Bullock, 1948
[11] Palmer, 1989
[12] ibid.
[13] Jennings, Researches

[14] ibid.
[15] Personal communication, June Palmer
[16] Tonkin, T., "The Great House", JRIC 1961
[17] Palmer, 1989
[18] ibid.
[19] ibid.
[20] Jennings, Researches & Palmer, 1989
[21] Duffin, 1996
[22] Gray, T., "Turks, Moors and the Cornish Fishermen", JRIC 1990
[23] Duffin, 1996
[24] Coate, 1963
[25] Palmer, 1989
[26] ibid.
[27] ibid.
[28] ibid. & North, C., "Fustians, Figs and Frankincense", JRIC 1995
[29] Palmer, 1989
[30] *Archaeological Investigations at City Hall, Truro, 1996*, Cornwall Archaeological Unit 1997 (Report commissioned by the Hall for Cornwall Trust)
[31] Palmer, 1989
[32] Dorling, 1982

Chapter 4

War, Suspicions and Rivalry

Charles I raised his standard at Nottingham on 22 August 1642 signalling the start of the Civil War. Which were the Burgesses of Truro to support, King or Parliament? All the signs seemed to show that Truro, like Plymouth and Exeter, would declare for Parliament. Truro's two MPs, John Rolle and Francis Rous, both supported Parliament's stand against the King. Francis Rous, described as "perhaps the most renowned of all men whose names are found on the burgess roll",[1] was the step-brother of John Pym, the main leader of the Parliamentary opposition at that time, and in 1640 they had led a debate on the grievances, especially religious ones, which they thought needed reforming. Lord Robartes, who still owned many properties in the borough, also supported Parliament. He had influenced the Truro elections in 1640 and had also prepared the attack on the King's chief adviser, Thomas Wentworth, which led to his execution. George Phippen, the rector of St Mary's church, was later to be imprisoned for his Parliamentary views, and nearby at Tregothnan, the Boscawen family also supported Parliament, with young Nicholas at once joining the Parliamentary army with a regiment of horse.[2]

Even before the King raised his standard, both sides in Cornwall were jockeying for control and trying to raise men and weapons for the coming fight. At first recruitment was slow. Many must have been reluctant to take sides and for some people getting in the harvest safely was much more important. When Royalist forces were called to a muster at Bodmin on 17 August very few turned up, and not one from Truro because the Mayor, Jacob Daniell, the son of Jenkin Daniell, refused to call out the Truro trained bands for the King. The time of year was soon approaching, however, for the appointment of a new Mayor.

Events moved more quickly towards the end of September when one of the King's professional soldiers, Sir Ralph Hopton, arrived in the county with cavalry troops. He went first to Stowe, the home of Sir Bevil Grenville (sometimes spelt Bevill Grenvile) near Kilkhampton, "one of the most popular men in Cornwall",[3] then on to Bodmin, after which he rode to Truro where he hoped he could "refresh his wearyed weather beaten men and horses and give a meeting to the well affected party in those parts."[4]

War, Suspicions and Rivalry

At this crucial juncture Sir Richard Vyvyan of Trelowarren, a Royalist, made a speech to the people of the Truro standing on the steps of the market house below the council chamber. We do not know all the details of his exhortation to the crowds of people who must have squeezed into the street, but he seems to have appealed to basic instincts, stressing the danger to their lives and to the lives of their wives and children if they did not obey the Sheriff and the Justices, who supported the King. With this appeal, helped maybe by the threatening or perhaps comforting presence of Sir Ralph Hopton and his men, the new Mayor, John Michell, agreed to allow the town's arms and men to be used for the King.

At this time there was no permanent army for either side to call on. Any man was liable for service in the militia and each county was supposed to supply men trained at the county's expense in times of emergency to defend their areas. The Truro trained bands, armed no doubt with muskets and pikes, now marched out of the town to face, not a foreign enemy but their own countrymen. These men of the militia, raised to defend their county, were reluctant to follow Hopton into Devon. To overcome this, volunteer armies were formed under five leaders including Sir Bevil Grenville, and Nicholas Slanning the Governor of Pendennis Castle. In Slanning's regiment was Captain Penwarne's Company which included many local men, among them Robert Jordan, Drummer, and at least fifteen others from Truro.[5]

No doubt news filtered back to the town during these first few months of the war of the campaigning around the county border with first the Royalists pushing into Devon and then the Parliamentarians forcing their way over the Tamar into east Cornwall. On one of these retreats Hopton wrote that the Cornish foot soldiers "had bene through the whole marche so disobedient and mutinous, as little service was expected from them if they should be attempted by the Enemy." However he was pleasantly surprised when, on being unexpectedly attacked, the men "put themselves into very excellent order of ready obedience beyond expectation."[6] He was to be even more impressed by their fighting qualities.

Truro, as a coinage and stannary town, was helping the king's cause, because although the mines were to suffer during the war, the sale of tin was an important source of money which could be used to buy weapons and gunpowder. Charles I's wife, Henrietta Maria, worked tirelessly in support of her husband organising the trade in munitions with her native country of France. The Royal Navy had declared for Parliament, so a fleet of ships established by Sir Nicholas Slanning was of vital importance. They not only acted as privateers preying

74

Anthony Payne, "The Cornish Giant",
painted by Sir Godfrey Kneller at the command of Charles II
in 1680. Plymouth in the background. (Courtesy RIC)

on merchant ships to seize their cargoes for the King's cause, but also transported the vital weapons. In the early months of the war these ships sailed into the Fal loaded with weapons and ammunition, so that by November 1642 Sir Nicholas and Francis Basset, who had the main responsibility for arming the new regiments, were able to supply 10,000 arms for infantrymen and 2,000 for cavalry along with 20 cannons.[7] The Parliamentarian Navy had orders not to go into the Fal, but in January 1643 storms drove three ships to take shelter there. This proved a windfall for the Royalists as the vessels were crammed with arms and money, so that the soldiers who fought at Braddock Down, the first main action of the war in Cornwall, were even better-armed, and happier with a fortnight's advance pay in their pockets.

After this battle Bevil Grenville wrote to his wife: "My Dear Love, It has pleased God to give us a happy victory, ... for which pray join me in giving God thanks." Bevil's charge had been particularly effective. He had led his yelling men down the slope and up the other side, his colours carried by his servant Anthony Payne, a giant of a man over seven feet tall. Nearly forty years later the portrait of this huge man reproduced on page 75 was painted by Sir Godfrey Kneller, and it can still be seen towering over visitors in the Royal Cornwall Museum in Truro.

These Cornish soldiers, nicknamed the "Cornish Malignants" by the opposition, were soon to gain a legendary reputation near Anthony Payne's home. The Parliamentarian army took a stand in what was thought to be an impregnable position on the top of a steep-sided hill near Stratton. Late on 15 May 1643 Hopton's army arrived tired, hungry and short of ammunition. He made his headquarters in the manor house at Stratton, which was Anthony Payne's birthplace, and attacked the following day. Against all the odds they rushed the hill on all sides until, as Hopton recalled, "the Commanders happened to meete altogether in one ground neere the Topp of the Hill, where having joyfully embraced one another they pursued their victorie, and recovered the topp of the Hill, which the Enimy had acquyted in a route."[8]

With morale high and Cornwall secure Hopton could now lead his troops through Devon and into Somerset, and soon news of more skirmishes began to reach Cornwall, followed by a battle at Lansdown near Bath, where once again the Cornish troops charged up a steep hill to victory, and then came the news of the capture of Bristol. But by this time the heart had gone out of many of the Cornish troops; the slaughter at Bristol was horrific and both Slanning and another commander were killed. Perhaps worst of all, Bevil Grenville had been killed at Lansdown. The story may not be true but it shows the emotions of the time, that as Bevil fell dead from his horse Anthony Payne swung his fifteen-year-old son, John, into his father's saddle so spurring the men on to victory.

King Charles' gratitude to the people of Cornwall at this time can still be seen on the wall of St Mary's Aisle in the Cathedral, because he sent a letter of thanks to the county which he wanted to be made known "in the most publick and lasting manner we can devise," by having copies kept in every church as a record "that as long as the History of these times and of this nation shall continue the memory of how much that County hath merited from us and our Crown may be preserved with it to Posterity." In the letter he referred to "the wonderful Success with which it hath pleased Almighty God (tho' with the Loss of some eminent Persons who shall never be forgotten by us) to reward their Loyalty and Patience by many strange Victories over their and our Enemies in despite of human probabilities, and all imaginable Disadvantages." One of these "eminent persons", Bevil Grenville, was not forgotten over 250 years later as his image can be seen in one of the stained glass windows of the Cathedral as well as his statue (right) on the south porch.[9]

Truro made another contribution towards this success besides being a coinage town and port for tin exports. For nearly a year the royal mint was churning out coins in Truro to provide

money to pay the soldiers as well as to buy food, weapons and ammunition. Sir Richard Vyvyan and Jonathan Rashleigh from Fowey were appointed by the King to collect silver plate sent in by supporters, and Sir Richard was given a commission to set up a mint to turn this plate into money wherever he chose. He chose Truro in the autumn of 1642, probably using the premises of John Parnell the goldsmith, which would have had the necessary furnaces and security, and with the goldsmith employed as the engraver. Half crowns of fine quality survive from this mint showing a victorious king on a lively horse trampling under its hooves pikes, halberds and muskets.[10]

Some people willingly gave their silver for the King's cause on security of 8%, such as Jonathan Rashleigh who recorded: "I brought soe much plate to be melted for the King's service at Trewroe as came to £104". Others could not stop their treasures from being taken as Lord Robartes discovered after Royalists had overrun his grand house of Lanhydrock. The Fowey Collector of Customs recorded charges for men and horses to carry "a truncke of the Lord Roberts his plate to Trewrow to the Mynt." Many towns gave the King their civic plate and it might have been expected that the Truro corporation would give up their two silver-headed maces. They were little more than twenty years old at the time, and perhaps it was through John Parnell's influence that these now venerable pieces of civic pride (shown below) were saved.[11]

The summer of 1643 had proved a fairly successful one for the King and, when Exeter was gained in September, all the south-west was safely his apart from Plymouth and Lyme Regis. At this point Sir Richard Vyvyan moved the mint from Truro to Exeter, which was now closer to the main campaigns, and there it remained for the rest of the war. Cornish people must have breathed a sigh of relief when the fighting moved away from the county that summer and there was only the garrison at Plymouth to worry about. But the following August parts of the county, especially around Lostwithiel, were to experience some of the bitterest fighting yet, along with the devastation caused by armies forced to live off the land, trampling crops into the ground, taking cattle and sheep and destroying or damaging houses. Some Truro people may have witnessed one sad, frightened woman who passed through their town that July fleeing the advancing Parliamentarian troops. Queen Henrietta Maria, who was doing so much to help her husband's cause, was forced to leave behind in Exeter her newly-born daughter as she fled to reach the safety of her native country. On 9 July, while in Truro, she wrote a letter to Charles, whom she was never to see again.

My dear heart,

This letter is to bid you adieu. If the wind is favourable I shall set off tomorrow. Henry Seymour will tell you many things from me, which the miserable condition I am in does not permit me to write. ...I am giving you the strongest proof of love that I can. I am hazarding my life that I may not incommode your affairs. Adieu my dear heart. If I die believe that you will lose a person who has never been other than entirely yours.

In spite of her weak state she still had the strength to ask for his help for some of the men who had assisted her.[12] She also gave a "thank-you" present to one of the Polwhele family who helped her: a locket set with diamonds and other jewels.[13]

The royal army, with the King at its head, was successful in Cornwall, although at some cost to the inhabitants, with the Parliamentarian commanders, Lord Essex and Lord Robartes forced to flee by boat while many of their men were left to suffer and die from starvation, exposure, disease or murder. But the king's forces had been routed in Yorkshire at Marston Moor by Oliver Cromwell's Eastern Association. Then, the newly-formed New Model Army, under the command of Thomas Fairfax and Oliver Cromwell, destroyed the King's hopes at Naseby in 1645. Before long it was making its inexorable way towards Cornwall.

Since January 1645 the king's eldest son, the fifteen-year-old Prince Charles, had been the titular head of the forces in the south-west. As the Parliamentarian forces advanced so he and his council were forced to retreat into Cornwall. In September Ralph Hopton and Edward Hyde, Charles' chief adviser, were surveying the defences of Pendennis Castle and inspecting the munitions at Truro to prepare a safe base for the Prince. From Truro that month, Sir Richard Grenville, an efficient but ruthless commander, had sent a letter to the Prince's Council citing Truro, Helston and St Ives as "the three most rotten towns in the west". By this time the Cornish people were being taxed beyond endurance, the tin mines, the chief source of wealth for many areas, were suffering from flooding and lost production, and undisciplined soldiers were causing offence. Richard's way of dealing with trouble in St Ives was to make a public display of hanging three of the men involved, one in each of these three "rotten" towns. In spite of this by the end of November Charles and his council had set up their headquarters in Truro.[14] Polwhele House and Lambessow have both been suggested as the Prince's residence during this time.

When Richard Grenville withdrew his forces without permission from Devon over the Tamar into Cornwall, it was to Truro that he was summoned to answer for his actions. There he suggested to the Prince that Cornwall should be a neutral zone and that Charles should negotiate a separate peace which would leave him free to enjoy the revenue from his Duchy. This plan was rejected but the situation was becoming desperate, for in spite of the winter and snowy conditions, Sir Thomas Fairfax was still advancing.[15] At the start of 1646 Ralph Hopton was given the supreme command of the Royalist forces in the west, replacing Grenville, but it was too late to heal divisions amongst commanders and to repair morale. The Parliamentarian victory at Torrington in February soon brought their army into Cornwall and the Prince and his council were retreating to the greater safety of Pendennis Castle. When Sir Thomas Fairfax reached Bodmin Charles, unknown to Hopton, left Pendennis for the Isles of Scilly. A boat had been prepared in readiness since the previous August for just such an emergency.

Hopton was forced to retreat to Truro where he still desperately resisted his officers pleas to negotiate with Fairfax. He knew that Pendennis Castle was still a viable stronghold which was garrisoned under the command of seventy-year-old Sir John Arundell of Trerice. He sent him a message offering to send down the river from Truro the stores and provisions still left in the town if Arundell could supply him with the boats. As Mary Coate has written: "The historian would give much for a minute book of the borough court of Truro, or for a diary by a local townsman of the events of these last days of the Royalist occupation, but no such records exist." Hopton was now prepared to surrender, but not to yield Pendennis.

Fairfax reported his progress to the Speaker of the House of Commons:

"I advanced with all the army from Bodmin toward Truro, being the enemies' headqurters, and to Tregony where I quartered that night Sir Ralph Hopton sent a trumpeter to me with a letter desiring to have commissioners on both sides to meet at Tresillian Bridge the next day with power to treat and conclude, which I assented to."[16] On 12 March 1646 the official surrender of the Royalist forces by Sir Ralph Hopton to Sir Thomas Fairfax was made at Tresillian Bridge, just east of Truro.

Fairfax commanded his soldiers to deal with the Cornish with restraint. Orders to his officers and soldiers written by him in Truro three days later and sent to the Royalist, John Polwhele, stated: "These are to require you, on sight hereof, to forebeare to prejudice John Polwhele, Esq. of Treworgan (an estate that came to the Polwhele's by marriage), either by plundering his house, or taking away his horses, sheepe or other cattell or goods, or by offering any violence to his person, or the person of any of his familie...provided he bee obedient to all orders of Parliament."[17]

Sir John Arundell and his garrison held out for another five months, but in August starvation and sickness finally forced them to surrender. They were allowed to march out in as fine a style as they could muster with drums beating, colours flying and the musketeers with bullets in their mouths and matches aflame. Pendennis Castle was then garrisoned by Parliamentary soldiers.

With the war now officially over, but with Charles I still alive, trouble again broke out in the west of Cornwall in 1648. Cornwall suffered badly at this time from poor harvests and outbreaks of plague especially in St Ives where perhaps half the population died. After the rioting had been dealt with the county came under a sort of military rule, as shown by John Taylor when he made his "Wandering to see the Wonders of the West" the following year.[18] He had been in royal service for 45 years with both Charles I and his father James and described this time as "dangerous days for Riche Men and miserable times for the Poore Servants of the late King", for Charles had been executed that January.

This man, who had already travelled in many other areas of the country often by boat and has been nicknamed the "Water Poet", wrote of this decade of the 1640s:

> *This is a mad world (my masters) and in sadness*
> *I travelled madly in these days of madness:*
> *Eight years a frenzy did this land molest,*
> *The ninth year seemed to be much like the rest,*
> *Myself (with age, grief, wrongs and wants opprest,*

War, Suspicions and Rivalry

With troubles more than patience could digest)
Amongst those ills, I chose the least and best,
Which was to take this journey to the West.

He found that every person was likely to be interrogated at the entrances to towns. They would be asked their name, where they lived, where they had come from, where they were going and what was the reason for their journey. "Now he that cannot answer these particular demands punctually is to be had before governors, captains, commanders, mayors or constables." Only then might he be allowed to go on his way and this he described as "a hazard of the loss of a traveller's liberty ... and at best it is a hindrance to a man's journey and a loss of time."

John Taylor passed through Truro in July on a day which started at St Enoder and ended at Redruth, eighteen miles in all, in which he saw nothing strange but some red-legged choughs. "They saluted me upon the wing, just in the langue of our jackdaws about London, Ka ka." However he stopped long enough in Truro "which is the Lord Roberts his land", to eat his dinner. The bream he was given for three pence "would have served four men."

"One of the best harbours for shipping in the world" was his description of the haven of the Fal when he reached Penny-come-quick, as the small settlement there was then called. He looked at Pendennis Castle but only from a distance, because he was afraid that he might be mistaken for a spy, as the examination of people near a garrison was even stricter. (Peter Mundy, a Penryn man, also made a pointed reference to this garrison stronghold: "This castle is become famous nowadaies. It is about 2½ miles from Penrin and many wish it were farther off in these tymes, anno 1650.")[19]

Royalist plots were constantly being feared during these troubled years. Strangers continued to be looked on with suspicion and were likely to be interrogated. This fear could be increased if the stranger also belonged to one of the religious sects that now emerged. The Parliamentarians had done away with the Anglican Prayer Book, but since there was no official replacement, different forms of worship were adopted, not all welcomed by the authorities. Dorothy Waugh, a Quaker, discovered this when she came to visit her friend Susan Daniell in Truro. She ended up in prison, put there by the Mayor. Some Quakers would infuriate local ministers by standing silently in church with their hats on and then perhaps interrupt the service. Even locally-known Friends could be brought before the authorities for this as Edward Hincks discovered in 1657. He was the leading Quaker in Truro and was put in prison "for coming into ye Church so called at Truro and for speaking to John Tingcombe priest". His stay in prison was very short, however, because they were afraid that his many children would become a charge on the town rates.[20]

Anna Trapnell, an Anabaptist, also found herself in trouble when she made a journey westwards from London in response to an invitation to visit Cornwall. She agreed very reluctantly and only when she felt that God wanted her to go. We have only her account, published in 1654, of what happened to her in Truro, but she seems to have caused a great stir in the town.[21] Her invitation had come from a Captain Langdon and his wife, who were living not far from Truro, at Tregassow in St Erme parish, and her account shows the continued presence of the army in the area, some of whom, like Captain Langdon, seem to have supported her. It was the magistrates and some clergy who feared her influence and suspected her of spreading discontent about the Government, which she flatly denied.

Her first visit to Truro came about a week after her arrival at Tregassow when she wanted to hear one of the sermons that were being preached in the town every three days. She was then invited back to dinner by a local couple, Mr and Mrs Hill. Anna was an unusual woman and her fame had obviously spread because many people wanted to see her, some perhaps for spiritual reasons and some just out of curiosity. For three years she had had visions, sometimes going into trances, and would sing and pray to extraordinary effect. There must have been a real buzz in the town about this strange person, and as soon as she had returned to Tregassow the clergy were calling her an imposter and a dangerous deceiver.

On her second visit to the town, where she stayed with Mrs Hill, she heard that warrants had been issued for her arrest. She worried about what she would do and say to the magistrates "having never been before any in that kind to be accused by them." She was then visited by two clergymen, one whose words were "but clergie-puff" and one who had ridden ten miles to see her and prayed with her "very sweetly and spiritually."

The following day she felt weak, went to bed and seems to have fallen into one of her trances. While she was "singing praises to the Lord for his love to me", the Justices sent the Constable to arrest her. However much he shouted, pulled and prodded her he could not get her to wake up, as he had to report to the magistrates. They obviously thought that this was all a trick to foil their questionings and insisted that she must be got out of bed unless anyone could swear an oath that this would endanger her life. No-one could, so they came to get her themselves.

What a scene there must have been as they strode through the streets to the house followed by their men and no doubt crowds of expectant onlookers! They stormed into the house and up to her room making "a great tumult" and when one man tried to stop them he was thrown down the stairs and beaten up by one of the magistrate's men. They hustled her friends out of the room then tried to wake her, convinced that she was just pretending. They pulled up an eye-lid, pinched her nose, tugged the pillow out from under her head, shouted and pulled, but all to no avail, and they had to leave angry but defeated. When she woke up two hours later she found herself alone and "blessed God for that quiet still day I had."

Not surprisingly the suggestion was being made by some that she was a witch and that the "witch-tryer woman" should be sent for "with her great pin" which she thrust into people to test them. Towards the end of the Civil War there had been a wave of witch hysteria in parts of the country, especially connected with the Parliamentarian General, Matthew Hopkins, and many people, women in particular, were found guilty of witchcraft and hanged. Although the Truro area seems from this account to have had a witch-finder little is recorded of cases in Cornwall during these years except for one at St Teath in 1645. A nineteen-year-old girl was accused of witchcraft and confined in Bodmin Gaol for a time by the magistrate, John Tregeagle, before being discharged.[22] One of the Justices who was to interrogate Anna was "a Mr Tregagle". Could this be the same magistrate, and was he the legendary bogeyman of Cornwall (historically Lord Robartes' steward) whose spirit was brought back from hell and who was condemned to empty Dozmary Pool with a sea shell?

Suspicion and surreptitious spying were rife in Truro that evening. Although the magistrates left Anna alone, many people came to the house, some to catch her out as she believed. That night her friends spent the time praying for her, but watched carefully what words they used because there were listeners under the window eager to pick up anything which could be used against them. She could not put off her ordeal any longer, because the following day the constable came to escort her to the "Sessions house". She had to make her way along the street through a jostling crowd of people, men and women, boys and girls, all eager to witness the excitement. Some were unfriendly, tugging at her arms, pulling faces at her, staring hard into her face and mocking her. When she reached the court room it was filled to overflowing "so that I was a gazing-stock for all sorts of people."

There she found herself standing below the group of Justices who were leaning over a rail looking down at her "with grim, fierce looks". A minister was also in attendance: "but though he and the witch-trying woman looked steadfastly in my face, it did no way dismay me." Justice Lobb, "the Mouth of the Court" as she described him, then read out the indictment against her to which she replied, instructed as she believed by God, "Not guilty." She was bound over to appear at the next Assizes on the surety of both her host, Captain Langdon, and a Major Bawden. But this was not the end.

It was believed by many that she would prove herself to be a witch by being unable to answer for herself to the magistrates, but as she said, "the Lord quickly defeated them herein." The Justices began to interrogate her on her reasons for coming to Cornwall and she showed herself very able in her replies, asking them why she should not come there and refusing to implicate her hosts for their invitation to her. Lobb commented then: "I understand you are not married." Her reply was: "Then having no hindrance, why may not I go where I please, if the Lord so will?" And so the questions continued.

At one stage two women were to be called to witness against her. Only one appeared but thought better of it when Mrs Grosse, "a gentlewoman of the town" who was standing next to her, reminded her that a false oath was a dangerous thing. (The Grosse family were wealthy merchants in Truro.) With that the woman turned and ran out of the court. The sympathy of at least some of the spectators was obviously with Anna by this time. A soldier in the court was seen smiling "to hear how the Lord carried me along in my speech" and this incensed one of the magistrates who tried to order him from the room for laughing at the court.

In the end Anna was allowed to return to the Langdons' house, but about ten days later soldiers came to arrest her. She was returned to London for trial and spent some time in prison there. This treatment did not stop her from returning to Cornwall in 1656. As she had written: "I bless the Lord, my sufferings are for righteousness sake, and I go not about to vindicate myself, but Truth."

Magistrates had their powers increased in 1653 by officiating at civil marriages, which were now allowed for the first time, and a "Registry Office" was set up in Truro. An entry in the parish register for St Mary's church in November 1653 states: "Wee the Mayor and Burgesses and other inhabitants of the town and borough of Truro doe hereby declare that we have made choice of John Bagwell to be Register of this town." A church ceremony was still allowed and the number of marriages taking place in Truro soared dramatically with John Bagwell recording all the civil ones. The first couple to be married in this way, with Jacob Daniell Esquire, Justice of the Peace, officiating, were

Richard Garland of St Veep and Mary Bramst of the parish of Veryan. Many of the young people came from outside the town and this perhaps indicates not so much the popularity of civil marriage ceremonies as the shortage of clergymen in many of the parishes.

Many of the Anglican clergy had been ejected from their livings and there were not enough Presbyterian and Independent ministers to replace them. Francis Rous, the MP for Truro for some of this time, was one of the commissioners appointed for ejecting "scandalous ministers and ignorant schoolmasters." John Tingcombe, Truro's minister, was concerned about the shortage and put it down to poverty. He did not have the tithes that rectors had benefited from in the past; he had to pay out £15 to repair the small parsonage when he moved in because it was in such a ruinous state and he was paying taxes of £3-4 a year on it. This highlights one of the reasons for the unpopularity of the Commonwealth rule: the high taxes that had to be levied on people partly to pay for war against England's trade rivals, the Dutch and the Spanish. It is perhaps significant that in Oliver Cromwell's last Parliament, in 1656, the representative for Truro was the barrister-at-law, Walter Vincent, "a clever, upright, popular man" and a known Stuart supporter.[23] In 1658 he represented Truro again, this time with Charles Boscawen, the first one of that family to become an MP for the borough which it was to influence for almost the next two hundred years. In 1660 many people were only too happy to welcome back Charles II from his exile.

Peter Mundy, the well-travelled Penryn man, was in London at this time and described the rejoicings on 29 May when Charles made his entrance into the City. "The bells ring out, the conduits run with wine but not a pistol shot is heard: only from the ships and from Tower Hill the ordnance thundered: at night bonfires ended the day's public triumph." No doubt Truro had its own celebrations, and for many years people wore an oak apple on this day in remembrance of the oak tree that had once sheltered the young Prince ten years earlier from Parliamentarian soldiers. (At St Neot an oak bough is still raised to the top of the church tower on this day.)

Many churches had been damaged during the war and then "simplified" in the following years, with the destruction of images or anything else that might encourage idolatry, so stained glass, Easter sepulchres, figures on tombs and other decorations were demolished or scarred. The grandmother of the historian, Richard Polwhele, told him that the rebels destroyed all the tombs and tablets where they could in the churches in and around Truro. The damage to St Mary's church seems to have been extensive from the amount of repair work that now got under way, once John Tingcombe had been removed and his successor Josias Hall instituted in 1662. The walls, roof and the stone work of the windows were repaired, windows were glazed, the tiles limed and new seats and iron work installed. The pulpit cloth was mended and washed as were the surplices, which had probably not been used by Tingcombe. The total cost in one year 1662-3 was over eighty pounds, a very significant sum.[24]

This church was remembered by a native of Truro, John White, who had made his fortune in London, but could so easily have lost it all again. In his will he left money for a sermon to be preached at St Mary's every year on 2 September "in acknowledgment of God's great mercy, who...preserved so great a part of the city from the devouring flames, which was on that day in the year 1666 kindled in the midst of the City of London..." The considerable amount of property that he had acquired in London had escaped the ravages of the Great Fire because the wind had changed just at the right time.

Persecution of minority groups still continued after the Restoration, as the Truro Quakers soon discovered. They recorded accounts of people arriving for their meetings at Edward Hinck's house, which was just in Kenwyn parish near where Victoria Square is today, and being violently thrown out by the Kenwyn constables and their men, having their clothes torn, being dragged along the street and stoned by boys. On top of this they could be fined for attending illegal meetings and Edward was fined £20 for allowing his house to be used. In the end the threats and violence lessened and they were finally left alone to hold their meetings in comparative peace in a house near the bottom of Chapel Hill.[25]

The rights of the Corporation came under threat at the end of Charles' reign with many town charters, including Truro's, being recalled by the King in 1684. No new one was issued until the following year, by which time his brother James had succeeded him. James, a convert to Roman Catholicism, wanted to increase Catholic influence in the country and needed a compliant House of Commons. Before long eight of Truro's Capital Burgesses found themselves dismissed for "misbehaviour" and the rest of the corporation accepted James' eight replacement nominees, which included one of the Roman Catholic Arundells, "a proceeding on the part of the Crown as disgraceful as can well be imagined and still more disgraceful on the part of the Mayor and Capital Burgesses who ought all have resigned rather than to have lent themselves to such an act of injustice to their colleagues."[26] The Capital Burgesses soon proved to be not quite so compliant after all, because when it came to the time to elect their two Members of Parliament, one was John Arundell but the other

was Henry Vincent, one of the dismissed Burgesses. After James' forced abdication in 1688 the Elizabethan charter was restored and remained in force for the next 147 years, until 1835.

During these years in the second half of the seventeenth century Truro's position as the chief town and port of the Fal was rivalled by both Penryn and Falmouth. The port of Penryn had been a threat for many years and in 1650 Peter Mundy had written that it was increasing in wealth, building and population "and may now compare with Truro." Twenty years later Charles II was prepared to grant to Penryn the right of coinage because much of the tin was being mined in parts of the stannary "remote from Our Coynage Towne of Truro" and this caused problems because of the narrow and steep roads which "will be of great inconvenience and charge to our Tynners to enforce them to carry all their Tyn to Truro...especially in the Winter season."[27] Truro and the other coinage towns fought off this threat temporarily, but twelve years later, in 1682, John Foote, Truro's Town Clerk, was ordered to go to London "to make the best defence that he can before the Lords of the Treasury in opposition to the making of the Burrough and Towne of Penryn a Coynadge Towne."[28] The fight against Penryn's influence was successful but the growth of the new town of Falmouth was another matter.

The castle at Pendennis gave protection to the bay and the estuary of the Fal but there was little else in the area at the beginning of the seventeenth century except the manor of the Killigrews at Arwenack. Peter Mundy, who was born about 1597, could remember when Falmouth was called Penny-come-quick and "there was but one house there." But the Killigrew family had other ideas and in James I's reign they had petitioned to have a customs house. Truro, Penryn and Helston all objected and Truro's fears could be seen when the Heralds visited in 1620 to confirm the Town Seals. The last paragraph of their confirmation stated: "Wee finde also that the maior of Truro hath always beene and still is Maior of Fallmouthe; as by an ancient graunt now in the custodie of the said Maior and Burgesses doth appeare."[29] But Truro was fighting a losing battle.

The Killigrews' support of Charles I was rewarded by his son who gave

---

Opposite: Early 19th-century engraving showing Truro's Town Quay,
completed in 1676.
Lemon Bridge and New Bridge, both seen in the picture,
were built later than the Quay.
(Courtesy RIC)

the small settlement a charter in 1661 to be called "by the name of our Town of Falmouth", and the church built soon afterwards was dedicated to King Charles the Martyr. Towns on the coast had earlier suffered from the raids of the Barbary pirates, but during the time of the Commonwealth Admiral Blake had not only defeated Dutch and Spanish fleets, but had also successfully attacked the pirates in their own waters. Falmouth could prosper, and when the Post Office chose Falmouth as its port to start a packet service in 1689 there was no looking back.

During the 1670s and 1680s the numbers of vessels entering the Fal increased dramatically and Truro also shared in this. It imported much more coal from South Wales, timber from London or Scandinavia, iron from Spain, Gloucestershire and Sussex and charcoal from the New Forest. This increased trade called for better facilities and in 1676 building work was completed for Truro's Town Quay where the Kenwyn and Allen rivers meet, which linked existing smaller quays.[30] By the 1680s nearly half of the county's exports, mostly tin, were passing through Truro, so the rise of Falmouth did not seem too damaging at first.

The coinage system had been abolished for a few years during the time of the Commonwealth. A pamphlet of 1654 stated: "There is no necessity for reviving the old way of coynages, since all the Tynne is and hath been for several years past, coyned and stamped at the blowing house by the Officers of Excise with the Commonwealth arms."[31] With the restoration of the monarchy in 1660 the old way was brought back. Some people tried to evade the duty. In 1695 the Mayor, William Gribble, complained that Henry Hearle was defrauding the King. Hearle, like others, had set up "kettles" in his private cellar under pretence of remelting into bars tin that had been coined, but he was in fact illegally melting uncoined tin. This offence did not prevent him from being elected Mayor on two later occasions.[32]

After the Restoration tin production increased. In the last years of the Commonwealth about one-and-a-half-thousand hundredweight of tin was exported from Truro. This soared to over fifteen-thousand hundredweight in 1667 and then increased still further.[33] In 1663 William Gregor, a Truro merchant, coined more tin than anyone else in the county, and another merchant from the borough, Thomas Cox, had the third highest amount.[34] Between 1663-1684 Truro coined on average over sixty percent of all the tin in the county, with Helston second in importance a long way behind on nearly eighteen percent.[35] In addition copper began to be mined on a large scale and with copper mines near Truro the town again benefited in spite of Falmouth. But this prosperity depended solely on the mines. If the mines fell on hard times then so would Truro.

In the 1690s bad harvests caused corn prices to rocket, and at the same time the mines suffered from a depression because of wars in Europe which lasted until 1713. Truro's trade with the continent fell sharply with consequent unemployment. Truro's tin exports plummeted from twenty-two thousand hundredweight in 1682 to about eleven thousand in 1696 and then even more disastrously to two-and-a-half-thousand hundredweight in 1698.[36] The town quay became ruinous and the streets were left unrepaired and dangerous for pedestrians. House prices fell, some buildings were left empty and the famous hostelry, the Bull Inn, closed down. Further bad harvests increased the problems, provoking food rioting in 1700, when people broke into a house in Truro and carried away 200 sacks of wheat.[37]

Celia Fiennes, a relation of the Boscawens at Tregothnan, gave a rather sad picture of the town at this time when she visited it on her travels "Through England on a Side Saddle". "Truro ... is a pretty little town and seaport, and formerly was esteemed the best town in Cornwall; now is the second, next Lanston." She then added, "... this was formerly a great trading town and flourished in all things, but now as there is in all places their rise and period, so this, which is become a ruinated disregarded place."[38]

The picture seems grim and some people thought that the town would never recover. In 1709 the Borough of Truro had to accept that its boundary as a port was no longer at the mouth of the Fal as it had traditionally claimed. A court case ruled that the port extended to Carrick Roads but stopped at a line stretching from Penarrow Point in Mylor to Messack Point in St Just, beyond which was the bustling new port of Falmouth. (Inscribed granite posts still mark this boundary.) In 1724, when Daniel Defoe was touring the country, he painted a pessimistic picture of Truro's future. "The town is well built, but shows that it has been fuller, both of houses and inhabitants than it is now; nor will it probably ever rise while the town of Falmouth stands where it does, and while the trade is settled in it as it is." But the copper and tin mines near Truro, which Celia Fiennes visited, were after all to prove Truro's salvation, and this town "built of stone" at the bottom of hills so steep "that you would be afraid of tumbling with nose and head foremost" was to prosper as never before.

References

[1] Jennings, P., "The Parliamentary History of Truro", JRIC XIV

War, Suspicions and Rivalry

2Gill, C., *The Great Cornish Families*, Cornwall Books, 1995
3 Coate, 1963
4 Wicks (ed.), 1988
5 Peter, T.C., "Sir Nicholas Slanning's Regiment in the Great Civil War", JRIC 1914
6 Wicks (ed.), 1988
7 Coate, 1963
8 Wicks (ed.), 1988
9 Personal communication on WEA course
10 Dorling, 1982
11 ibid.
12 Jennings, Researches
13 Polwhele, 1826
14 Coate, 1963
15 ibid.
16 Jennings, Researches
17 Polwhele, 1826
18 Taylor, J., *Wandering to See the Wonders of the West*
19 Keast (ed.), 1984
20 Palmer, 1989
21 Taprell, Anna, *A Defiance...* (available on microfilm at RIC)
22 Jones, K., *Witchcraft in Cornwall*, Sir Hugo Books, 1995
23 Jennings, P., "The Parliamentary History of Truro 1469-1660", JRIC XIV
24 Bullock, 1948
25 Palmer, 1989
26 Jennings, Researches
27 Henderson, C., Calendar No.9
28 Jennings, Researches
29 Dorling, 1982
30 Sheppard, 1980
31 Jennings, Researches
32 Jennings, P., "The Mayoralty of Truro 1538-1722", JRIC XVI
33 Whetter, J., "Cornish Trade in the Seventeenth Century", JRIC 1964
34 Whetter, 1974
35 ibid.
36 ibid.
37 Palmer, 1989
38 Gibson (ed.), 1968

Chapter 5

A Town of Merchant Princes

At the end of the eighteenth century, one hundred years after Celia Fiennes' rather depressing description of Truro as a "ruinated disregarded place", another traveller to the borough, James Forbes, gave a very different picture. "I have seldom seen a neater town than Truro; the best streets wide and airy, with good houses and well furnished shops, all paved in the modern style ... Everything here seems improving, and nothing going to decay."[1] Another visitor at this time in the 1790s was W.G.Maton, who described Truro as "unquestionably the handsomest town in Cornwall". He then added: "More tin and copper are exported hence than from any port in the county."[2] The eighteenth century saw not only a resurgence in tin mining, but most spectacularly a massive increase in copper mining, with Truro benefiting from both.

It was not only as a port, coinage and stannary town that Truro was connected with the mining industry. Maton's account continued: "About one mile and a half from Truro, on the road to Falmouth, there is a large smelting-house for tin. It contains ten reverberatory furnaces, which employ about twenty men. Culm-coal is used as the flux ..." This was the smelting works at Calenick established in 1711, which, with its predecessor at Newham, was amongst the first to use a new method of smelting tin, using coal rather than charcoal. So it was close to Truro that this revolution in tin smelting first became a commercial proposition in the early years of the eighteenth century.

Charcoal, the traditional fuel for smelting, had become scarcer and scarcer in Cornwall during the seventeenth century as woods were being destroyed and not replanted. Cornish mines were depending increasingly on charcoal from the New Forest, which was expensive. Experiments began using the cheaper coal from South Wales and one of the experimenters was Robert Lydall, described as a "gentleman of Truro".[3] He was granted two patents: the first in 1702 was for his "New Way of Smelting and Melting Black Tinn into good merchantable White Tinn, in a Reverbatory Furnace, without the help of Bellows ..." The second patent, granted three years later, stated more precisely the source of power for the smelting: "Culm and Sea Coal, in a Blast Furnace called *Ignifurens* ..."[4] and it stressed that this method was much cheaper than any other.

*Looking across the bridge to Calenick Smelting Works after its
closure in 1891 (Courtesy Royal Cornwall Polytechnic Society)*

Behind cob walls, in great secrecy, new furnaces were built at Newham
just beyond the Truro borough boundary, close to the river, where boats could
bring in the coal (culm) from South Wales and where Lydall may already have
had a smelting works. This project was financed by London merchants who
bought the patent and had six furnaces installed under his directions, four in
"the old workhouse" and two in a new building.

The Account Book indicates the scale of the new buildings that were
soon being erected, including a wainscoted counting house, costing £20, an
assay office, a 60-foot shed, new warehouses with hutches for storing the
black tin, a smith's shop, a kettling house, a house for making bricks and a
carpenter's shop, while in the "orchard" stamps, buddles and water courses
for processing the tin were installed. In addition there were stables, and a
buttery presumably for feeding the workmen. Strict rules were laid down for
the behaviour of the workmen. If a man was found drunk at work, or hit
another man, he would be fined a day's wages. That would amount to 1s for a
labourer or 1s 4d for a carpenter. If a man was found sleeping, heard cursing
and swearing, or abusing another workman "with vile base or unworthy names",
he would be fined 6d. The Account Book also shows the expenses involved in

coinage. For the Midsummer coinage of 1705 there had been 2s 6d to pay the barrowmen, 1s 6d for both the shouldermen and the cutters, 2s for the poiser's men who worked the scales, 6d for both the numerator and the doorkeeper, as well as 12s "spent with coynage officers at Newham" and frequent mentions of standing treat at "ye Ship", "King's Head", "Red Lyon" and "ye Coffee House at Truro."[5] Perhaps "standing treat" was especially important for a new process that had to prove itself.

By November 1704 the stamps were working day and night and this enterprise was soon prospering. This caused consternation among the owners of the traditional blowing houses, at a time when the European wars were still creating some problems for the industry. Soon rumours began to circulate that the tin produced at Newham was of much poorer quality than normal. In addition it was supposed to have been adulterated with other metals, and the account book certainly shows a suspicious amount of "white mundick" being bought. Robert Lydall was said to have left in protest, but he may have left to set up new smelting works at Angarrack, near Hayle, for the same company.

The Crown Agents for managing the tin contract in Cornwall led the agitation against this new process and various tests were carried out, officials from the Royal Mint becoming involved. In the end the Newham tin passed the tests in spite of all the efforts made to stop the enterprise. Soon after, in 1711, the Newham proprietors moved their main premises to Calenick, where they already had stamps for breaking up the hard lumps of slag, perhaps because there was a better supply of running water from the Nansavallon stream. There it remained as one of the main tin smelting houses of Cornwall until 1891.

Soon others were trying to fight this monopoly including one Truro man, Samuel Enys. He was establishing himself as one of the most powerful men in the borough having recently inherited the wealth of both his grandfathers, Samuel Enys, an astute Penryn merchant, and Henry Gregor, one of the most important merchants in Truro in the later seventeenth century. In 1706 Samuel bought the Manor of Kenwyn and Truro, so acquiring much land in and around the town, he invested in mines, and amongst other enterprises he was a partner in a blowing house at Treyew, about a mile higher up the Nansavallon valley from Calenick. In 1711 he became the sole leaseholder, and behind new high walls he began to build his own smelting house.[6]

Perhaps his actions were an early example of industrial espionage because the details of the new smelting process had been kept as secret as possible. So how did he gain the necessary technical knowledge? Samuel's uncle, Richard Enys, was one of the Crown Agents who had led the protest against the Newham works. He had been allowed into the works at one stage to look at the furnaces and had been able to talk to the men working there. Samuel also had other possible sources of information. One of his boyhood friends was Richard Plint, a goldsmith in the town, whose family home was at Newham. The works there had been built on land leased from Henry Plint, probably his father, who had also undertaken the making up of a road to the works and keeping it in repair. Samuel employed Richard at Treyew as assayer and also took on a brother, Henry, a pewterer, so between them they had a good knowledge of metal working. In addition Robert Lydall was also involved with Samuel in this enterprise. Samuel was soon being taken to court by the Calenick proprietors for poaching on their monopoly and enticing some of their workmen away to work for him.[7]

The dispute dragged on for over two years and in the end the case was possibly settled out of court. Samuel claimed that he was not breaking the monopoly because the methods he used were being practised for copper smelting at Polrudden twenty years earlier, before Lydall had been granted his patent. Not long afterwards he discovered that the Plint brothers were defrauding him and perhaps because of this he disposed of the Treyew lease, which was only one small part of his prosperous business enterprises.[8]

Samuel built for himself a new house right in the heart of the trading activity of Truro, with land backing on to the River Allen where he established his own quay. Here he was close to the Coinage Hall and the Town Quay, and from his elegant, sashed windows he could keep an eye on all the shipping movements. This house, whose front door is pictured right, still stands in Quay Street, much altered inside, but with its new-fashioned symmetrical, classical façade much as Samuel would remember, although he might disapprove of the plaster now covering the bricks which he had especially imported from London,

The Old Mansion House today, following renovations

an uncommon feature in the town at that time. The Old Mansion House, as it is now called, still contains some of the wood panelling and the plaster work that decorated the walls and ceilings of his modest-sized rooms; a restrained rather than a flamboyant display of wealth.

Samuel also indulged in some of his sporting passions, hunting and cockfighting. He kept a pack of hounds in kennels in Goodwives Lane and built a cockpit behind Pydar Street.[9] His account book for December 1708 records: "To Tabbs for tileing of New House & Cockpitt walls £5.01.00." In January and March the following year there were payments to two other men for work on the cockpit, and on April 7 1709 these two entries were added: "for 6 trees set

Old Mansion House—an SOS order

CARRICK District Council have made a compulsory purchase order for the Old Mansion House in Quay-street in a bid to save the oldest listed building in Truro city centre from further decay.

Mr. Alan Rigby, the council's deputy planning officer, told the "Argus" that the building has been empty since 1980.

It was bought by Unicorn Bluechip Investments, a Guernsey-based company. "They fairly quickly got out of a scheme for a gentlemen's club and there was a lot of activity," said Mr. Rigby.

"After being empty for five years the building is deteriorating, and the council have a duty to see that listed buildings are kept in good repair," said Mr. Rigby.

Article from West Briton Argus, *May 1985*

in cockpit £1 19s 2d" and "to dunge for trees 6d."[10] In 1710 he persuaded the Corporation to lease him the land between the front of his house and the Green for a surprising 999 years, where in later years the inn called "The Fighting Cocks" was operating, and here he may have built his own personal cockpit.[11]

In his pessimistic description of Truro's situation in 1724 Daniel Defoe wrote: "the trade is now in a manner wholly gone to Falmouth, the trade at Truro being now chiefly (if not only) for the shipping off of block tin and copper ore, the latter being lately found in large quantities in some mountains between Truro and St Michael's" (Mitchell).[12] He seems to have underestimated the significance of this trade, but Samuel Enys was too astute to have established himself in a town with poor prospects.

Another man who also felt that Truro was a town with a bright future, and who was becoming increasingly involved with copper and tin mining as well as with most other aspects of the industry, was William Lemon, who arrived in Truro soon after Defoe's visit and made it his home. He was probably then in his late twenties and had already begun to make a name for himself. As a very young man he had been one of the managers of the Chyandour tin-smelting works near Penzance, and Richard Polwhele, the Cornish historian, believed that he started off as a clerk to Mr Coster where "he had the best opportunities of making observations on the conduct of our mining adventurers and all their concerns."

John Coster from the Forest of Dean, who has been described as the "Father of Cornish Copper Mining",[13] had started a copper smelter near Monmouth and later took on the lease from the Boscawens of the Chacewater Mine, a few miles from Truro. Copper ore was usually found at a deeper level than tin so drainage in the mines was a perennial problem. Coster and his son John extended the use of drainage adits, patented an improved water wheel for raising water and introduced the horse whim to Cornwall which could raise water from deeper levels than with the usual manpower. Working for them provided the young William Lemon with a good opportunity to see for himself how these problems could be tackled and in due course he became one of Mr Coster's partners in the Gwennap mines. "He was the first who conceived the project of working the mines upon the grand scale on which they are at present conducted," wrote Richard Polwhele.[14]

His willingness to think big and to take calculated risks had been shown in 1720 when he brought into Cornwall the Devon engineer, Thomas Newcomen, to set up one of his new steam pumping engines, one of the first in Cornwall, to drain water from Wheal Fortune in the parish of Ludgvan. William Lemon's

"The Great Mr Lemon" - from a painting at the Royal Cornwall Museum

share in the profits of this mine were said to be about £10,000, not a bad start for a young man in his mid twenties making his own way in the world. His capital was further increased by his marriage in 1724 to Isabella Vibert from Gulval, and it was some time after this that the couple arrived in Truro to live, at first in Church Lane, now Cathedral Lane, a few minutes walk away from Pydar Street where the Costers leased a property.[15] He was soon to be regarded as one of the most influential men of the county.

In his youth he had shown great strength, bravery and leadership when he had led a human chain through raging surf to rescue sailors from a ship wrecked on the rocks near Praa Sands.[16] In his later life he was described by Richard Polwhele as being "a fine commanding person" admired for his ability rather than loved for his personality. In Truro people were said to draw back from their windows and doors as a mark of their respect when he passed in the streets. "To him people of all ages looked up, with a degree of awe. His approach occasioned a sensation." He must have cut a very impressive figure in the town wearing his silver-mounted sword and riding on his fine horse with its gold-trimmed saddle and silver studded bridle, or sitting in his post-chaise (a rare vehicle in Cornwall at that time) drawn by its four matched chestnuts. On one occasion, when Richard Polwhele's father was entertaining the curate of St Mary's, Samuel Walker, and the schoolmaster, George Conon, they were discussing the undue deference shown to men of consequence when in walked William Lemon. Immediately they stood up "and bowed with all humility to the great man as if overawed by his presence."[17]

Both these men would have known William Lemon well and George Conon may have seen a more humble side to the great man. He visited William Lemon frequently in his later life, not just social calls, but to tutor him in the classical studies which his childhood education had lacked, for he was prepared to admit to his lack of knowledge and to ask for help from the schoolmaster. His ability at expressing himself in English was shown in his successful appeal to Robert Walpole (effectively the Prime Minister although that title was not then in use) for the removal of a duty on coal used for the mines, for which Walpole complimented him on the clear and able way he presented his arguments.

Often of an evening William Lemon and the curate, Samuel Walker, with some other local men, would go to Kenwyn Church to ring the bells for enjoyment. It must have given William further satisfaction knowing that these bells were there mainly because of his bounty. His relations with the curate, however, were not always cordial. In 1746 Samuel Walker had arrived in Truro, "the town of dissipation" as quoted by Polwhele, and through the

Nineteenth-century engraving of Kenwyn Church
(Courtesy Cornish Studies Library, Redruth)

influence of George Conon he began an evangelical ministry which gained him both fervent followers and intense opposition. His strong beliefs caused great upset when he refused to repeat the usual words of the funeral service, "in sure and certain hope of the Resurrection to eternal life", at the funeral service in 1749 of the Collector of Customs, Thomas Quarme, a man of "high Norman lineage", according to Polwhele, but of profligate habits. Polwhele states that Mr Lemon "took a decided part against Walker" over this. His dominating behaviour also upset another man. His grandson, Colonel John Lemon, told of a time when he "kicked out" Mr Thomas of Tregolls from the walk of the piazza at the Coinage Hall saying that it was "meant for gentlemen and not for a roguish attorney."[18]

His dealings with another Thomas, young John Thomas, put him in a more favourable light. The Cornish chough, which had earlier been remarked on by John Taylor the Waterman Poet, was still seen around Truro in William Lemon's time, and he had a particular favourite who would come at his whistle when he walked on the Green or in the streets, so this bird was regarded with some veneration by the townspeople. Imagine the consternation when John Thomas, a pupil at the Grammar School, disobeyed the rules and went out

101

with his gun on Back Quay and took a pot-shot at a group of birds. The chough fell down dead, and the boy was quickly surrounded by people prophesying the direst punishments for him once Mr Lemon found out, far worse than the flogging he was likely to get for breaking school rules. It must have taken considerable courage for him to walk up the grand steps and knock at the front door of Mr Lemon's house and then, when he was ushered into the presence of the great man himself, to admit to what he had done. William Lemon looked at his tearful face and not only forgave him for his candour but also promised not to report the incident to Mr Conon. Not only that but he also said that if the school master found out about it then he would intercede for him.[19] No doubt one very relieved boy was then shown out, who would have had little thought for the impressive house that he now thankfully left behind him.

William Lemon, who was made a Capital Burgess in 1731 and was twice chosen as Mayor, as well as being appointed Sheriff for the county, had built for himself a house that well-suited his social standing. Princes House, as it is now called, was close to the Coinage Hall and the quays and not far from the house that Samuel Enys had earlier built, but it was on a grander scale. (One of its ground-floor windows is shown in the photograph.) It had three reception rooms, the largest one, which overlooked the garden leading down to the Kenwyn River, having an ornate marble fireplace and a ceiling covered in rich plaster work. A wide mahogany staircase led up past more elaborate plasterwork to the spacious landing from which opened three bedrooms, each with its fourposter beds with damask curtains and chair covers in green, yellow or crimson.[20]

Much of the furniture was made from richly-coloured mahogany, a wood that had started to be imported in any great quantity only in the 1730s, so his fifty-six

102

*Princes House. The porch is a late nineteenth-century addition
by Silvanus Trevail.*

chairs, two dining tables, stools and mirror-frames, recorded in the inventory after his death, were right in the fashion of the times. William and Isabella Lemon were also up-to-date in having china which was beginning to replace pewter in the wealthier households of the day. They had two blue and white table sets, probably imported from China, with various dishes, tureens, soup and fruit plates and a large number of "common plates" indicating that they entertained on a large scale. These sets also included cups for drinking the new, fashionable and expensive beverages of chocolate, coffee and tea, and in addition they had two very elaborate tea sets decorated with gilt.

One can imagine Isabella Lemon entertaining the ladies after dinner in the drawing room sitting on the chairs with their flowered upholstery, talking of clothes, recipes, their difficulties with the wilful younger generation, or the shortcomings of their servants, while they drank their precious tea out of the small china cups. Sarah Gregor, a descendant of the Truro merchant family, who was born at the end of the eighteenth century, wrote that it was the correct thing to drink off the cupful and then hold "the beautiful ware to the light to admire its transparency at the bottom".[21] If this was true in her young days then how much more would these delicate Chinese cups have been admired fifty years earlier?

This impressive town house was not their only home because in 1748 William Lemon bought the Carclew estate a few miles south of Truro. Here he completed an unfinished house with a grand pillared portico and colonnades planned by the architect, Thomas Edwards, who had also designed Princes House. Parkland and gardens gave his family the space denied in the confines of the town, and this would have been their main residence, certainly during the summer months. The journey there might have taken them down the steep, narrow hill to Calenick, where he had recently acquired the smelting works to add to his business empire, which soon featured a clock tower that can still be seen outside Calenick House.

William Lemon, as befitting a Capital Burgess and Mayor, was active in the town and in its improvement, especially with the church. From about the 1740s changes were being made to the inside of this venerable building, including clearing out the old monuments, many still bearing damage from the time of the civil wars, and cartloads of stonework were taken out and dumped on the banks of the River Allen. One of the largest tombs was the impressive one of John Robarts and his wife. William Lemon was determined that this one would also go, but even more determined was Lord Radnor of Lanhydrock, their descendant, that it should stay. For once Mr Lemon lost this battle of wills.[22]

The tomb must have been in a very sorry state but it was not repaired for another fifty years when it was becoming a liability. In 1799 William Jenkin, the agent of the Agar-Robartes family, was asked by some of the Magistrates of the Borough to take a look at it. "It was a very handsome one but is now tottering into ruins," he wrote to Lanhydrock. "I suppose the Cramps which supported are failed, and it seems dangerous to sit or stand under it." He had immediate instructions to repair it and replied: "I take due notice of thy directions for repairing the Monument in Truro Church, and will get it done with as little expense as I can."[23] The reclining figures received new noses, hands, toes and buttons where needed, and it is now one of the most interesting monuments in the Cathedral.

In 1750 a new organ, the Byfield organ, which can still be seen in St Mary's Aisle, was installed, probably provided by William Lemon, and about the same time high-backed seats for the Corporation were placed in the centre of the church, no doubt to maintain the dignity of the Burgesses. A new pulpit was also installed, finely carved in wood, probably made by Henry Bone's father, a local carpenter and cabinet maker. Henry Bone, who was born in 1755, and who later moved with his family to Plymouth when he was about twelve years old, was to become well-known as a painter of enamels, a Royal Academician and painter for many of the Royal Family.

A visitor to Truro at this time, Dr Richard Pococke, remarked on the elegant church with the handsome tomb of the Roberts, and he also mentioned the old painted glass.[24] Five years later, when another traveller, William Wynne, visited the town, he commented on the church with its good organ, handsome pews and galleries (the north one of which was yet another example of William Lemon's influence), but by this time much of the glass had gone, to be used, so it is said, by children as toys.[25] William Wynne also praised the appearance of the town with its stone houses covered with blue slate and where "'tis common to see at merchants doors blocks of tin lye, that are worth £1000 or £1500 each of which block is worth £10."[26] It was wealth from both this tin and the copper ore that made all these changes to the church possible.

Changes were also being made on the outside of the church. In 1755 the base of what is believed to have been the medieval High Cross was taken away, which was all that was now left of this ancient relic. This had latterly been used for tying up a bull kept in the castle field for the sport of bull-baiting, but this form of entertainment had now gone out of fashion. The small graveyard to the south and east of the church was lowered and enclosed by iron railings and a considerable number of bones were dug up and dumped, with the wreckage of the stone monuments, on the banks of the river at the back of the Bear Inn. No doubt William Lemon was involved with these "improvements", and perhaps it was this that upset the sexton, Tristrem, who seems to have greatly disliked him. Whatever the reason for his strong feelings, which presumably he had to keep suitably under control when the great man was around, he saw no reason not to show his elation when William Lemon died in 1760. According to Richard Polwhele, the sexton "was ready to leap out of his skin for joy" and after the body had been interred he stamped on the vault and cried out: "Thank God! we've got him under now."[27]

With William Lemon dead there was a power vacuum. He should have been succeeded by his only son, another William, who was following in his father's footsteps, having been made a Capital Burgess in 1750, the year his father was Mayor for the second time, and only five years later he had also been chosen for that exalted position. "He gave promise of being a man of great business aptitude and had he lived, would doubtless have become one of the leading men of Cornwall".[28] But two years later, in 1757, when he was

Engraving of St Mary's church in 1802, showing the iron railings enclosing the south and east sides.The steeple was erected in 1769. Notice the early street lamp, probably fuelled by seal oil. *(Courtesy RIC)*

only thirty-three, he died, leaving a young widow and three children, two sons and a daughter, all under the age of ten. It was to be some years before the eldest one, yet another William, was old enough to make his mark on the town.

However, William Lemon had prepared another man capable of taking over some of his huge business empire. This was Thomas Daniell (probably descended from the Daniells of the early seventeenth century), who had begun working for William Lemon when he was about ten years old. Under his patronage he was educated as a merchant and later was to be named as one of the trustees of his will. In Polwhele's words both William Lemon and Thomas Daniell were men whose success came from "ingenuity and perseverance, and a bold adventurous spirit in mining and merchandise." Gilbert, another historian of the time, said of Thomas Daniell: "Through his unwearied exertions many of the Cornish mines have been kept at work for more than half a century which would otherwise have remained unwrought."

In his late thirties Thomas Daniell married Elizabeth Eliot, the niece of

Ralph Allen, the St Blazey man who had made a name for himself organising the cross-country postal system of the country, and had made a fortune both from this and his quarries near his home of Prior Park in Bath. It was with financial help from him that Thomas was able to take over some of the Lemon enterprises, amongst which was the Calenick smelting works, and to build up a very considerable fortune. With mine production increasing he probably built a quay at Point further down-river, for ships to bring in timber and coal for the mines and to carry copper ore across to the smelting works of South Wales.

*Thomas Daniell holding a sample of copper ore. This famous painting
by John Opie shows him with one of his mine captains.
(Courtesy RIC)*

Like William Lemon, Thomas seems to have been a good judge of men, because he employed as his chief clerk John Martyn, a Gwennap miner, who showed great mathematical ability and who, according to Richard Polwhele, "conducted himself to the satisfaction of his rich and generous patron".[29] With this help John was able to send his clever seven-year-old son, Henry, to the Grammar School, where his grounding in the ancient languages may well have helped him in his later missionary work in India and Arabia, translating the New Testament into Hindustani and Persian. While at school he scratched his name on a window with sentences in Greek, Latin and Arabic. This piece of glass was saved from the old school in later years, only to be destroyed when fire swept through the Municipal Offices in 1914. He is remembered in the Cathedral nowadays in the windows of the baptistry.

Thomas Daniell comes across as a much less awe-inspiring figure than "the Great Mr Lemon", being a popular man with a friendly and convivial manner. Richard Polwhele, who was a friend of his son, Ralph Allen Daniell, wrote of his "admirable punch, so much the attention of the Truro-folk and of strangers, who in the days of punch-drinking preferred it to all they had ever tasted in old England or Caledonia." He then described how with "ludicrous solemnity of countenance" Thomas, then an elderly man, prepared the drink, squeezing the lemons, flinging in the sugar and water, then adding a "smack" of sherbet, mixing these together before pouring in the rum "rendering sour, and sweet, and weak and strong, delicious in their blending."[30] This was obviously a serious and skilled performance.

Whether his guests would have been able to negotiate themselves out of the room successfully after this hospitality is difficult to say. Polwhele had memories of sliding over the polished mahogany floor "to the vast amusement of the tittering sex, who would have laughed to see me laid low." Perhaps it was this warming drink which attracted Dr Wolcot to be a frequent visitor. He lived nearby in one of Thomas Daniell's properties overlooking the Green,

now the Britannia Inn, rent-free Polwhele believed because of "the liberality of that good old gentleman", and he always welcomed him to his house where the "wit and pleasantry of (his) conversation made him an agreeable guest".[31] This wit often took a satirical turn and was definitely not appreciated by some of his victims; but more of this later.

Polwhele described Thomas Daniell's house as "unquestionably the best in Truro," and the beauty of the Mansion House can still be appreciated today. It was built close to William Lemon's impressive town house a few years after his marriage to Elizabeth, in about 1759 and was designed by the same architect as Princes House but with more refined, less flamboyant details. Although grey Cornish granite was used for the basement, most of the stone is pale gold in colour, being limestone from Uncle Ralph Allen's quarries, given to the young couple, perhaps as a late wedding present. The stone was transported by boat and unloaded on to Thomas's own quay on the Kenwyn river at the bottom of his garden.

A Town of Merchant Princes

Large bay windows, a new architectural idea of the time, with twin projecting walls running the full height of the house, gave Thomas and Elizabeth a fine view over their garden to the boats moored by their quay. On the other side of the house an impressive flight of steps led up from the road to the pillared doorway and so into a vestibule and small domed hallway, which then led into the main hall with its grand staircase and elegant wrought iron banisters: a fitting mansion for the man who was described as one of the most eminent merchants, tin smelter and above all, "a spirited adventurer in mines on the largest scale". No wonder Richard Polwhele described Truro as a town where "as in ancient Tyre, the tin glitters in its streets and all its merchants are princes."

Fanlight over the front door of the Mansion House

Henry Rosewarne, a close neighbour of Thomas's for some years, would have appreciated being described as a "merchant prince." "Large, domineering and ambitious" was June Palmer's description of him in *Truro in the Eighteenth Century*, and "the county's proudest mean-born fool" was Dr John Wolcot's less flattering comment. His wealth was based on mine adventuring, trading and tin smelting. His father, Walter, also a merchant, had taken over the lease of the Treyew smelting house for a time, but the main Rosewarne smelter was at Carvedras near the River Kenwyn just outside the town. Henry also bought up the Calenick works but, according to his wife, this was in order to keep it idle so that it did not provide unwelcome competition.[32] His influence was increased when he was appointed Vice-Warden of the Stannaries and helped to fix the price of tin when the war with America was creating difficulties for the industry. He seems to have been the only Vice-Warden who sold his shares in the mines on his appointment, realising that his new judicial position was not compatible with being an adventurer. The sale of his shares in nineteen mines was held at the Red Lion in April 1779. "A courageous step for, unlike his predecessors, he had inherited no landed estates from his father."[33]

In the 1770s he lived in what was often called the Great House, overlooking the bowling green at the corner of Princes Street, nowadays the premises of the Royal Bank of Scotland, from where he could see the river and watch the comings and goings of the merchants' ships. It lived up to its name, because it had four parlours, a large dining room, ten bedchambers, a kitchen and brew house, as well as a walled garden and a large stable.[34]

"The Great House" today, after many changes and renovations

Richard Polwhele, who lived there some years later, described one of the rooms as having "lofty doors and window-frames of mahogany, and

111

specimens of foreign marble in its chimney-piece (the most beautiful I ever saw)", and in all this he saw the influence of the wealthy merchant Henry Rosewarne, who in this house entertained "the first personages of the county". This hospitality was on a lavish scale with "grand concerts and splendid assemblies" and suppers which exhausted "all the luxuries of the season," but as the following lines from Dr Wolcot show, there could be an ulterior motive behind this display.

> *The best of good victuals his palace is rich in -*
> *Roast goose in the parlour and beef in the kitchen*
> *Gratis all - the votes call for whatever they please;*
> *So their hands and their chops are as busy as bees.*

In 1780, the year when he helped to fix the price of tin, he also increased his influence by becoming one of the two Members of Parliament for Truro.

The power struggle behind this election was fierce, partly caused by Sir Francis Basset of Tehidy trying to oust Boscawen influence in Truro. Lord Falmouth put forward two relations as candidates, who would normally have been accepted with little fuss. Rosewarne, helped by "his shadow", John Thomas, as H.L.Douch describes him in *The Book of Truro*, who was appointed Mayor in 1779, gained by various means so much control over the Corporation that they "persuaded" a majority to vote for him. (The election of MPs was still only in the hands of the Mayor and the twenty-four members of the corporation.) To Westminster with Henry Rosewarne went Bamber Gascoyne, who had already been representing the town, and Lord Falmouth's two candidates were both beaten, an unheard-of situation.

During these years of his power Rosewarne, as well as other members of the Corporation, were mocked by the satirical verses of Dr John Wolcot. The doctor had arrived in the town in 1772 to practise medicine, and at first his witty conversation made him welcome in many homes, but the victims of his satire became increasingly annoyed by his humour. He described Rosewarne:

> *A man with nose erect and eyes*
> *Forever pointed to the skies.* (From *The Hall*)

Polwhele criticised Wolcot for "being prompt in ridiculing the foibles of a truly respectable man," because there was far worse comment than this. In *A Christmas Carol*, supposedly quoting Atty White, the town crier, he wrote:

> *About twenty years since, both the men and the women*
> *Swore no mortal alive could compare with old Lemon:*
> *But now from our Magistrates gladly we learn*
> *That old Lemon's a blockhead to Master Rosewarne.*

Later in the same poem came this verse:

A Town of Merchant Princes

> So great is his power, that, without asking for 't,
> He rides in his coach through the turnpikes for nort;
> And though 'tis a theft for which well we might try 'un,
> The commissioners all are afraid to deny 'un.

And then:

> So great is his credit, he makes London town
> Believe all the tin that's in Cornwall his own;
> E'en a taylor that made 'un a jacket and coat
> Trusted Master Rosewarne without asking his note.

He ended with this verse:

> Then Truro bow down to this second Colossus,
> Whose greatness and cunning so deeply engross us;
> Let us sing to his praise, though the county divide us-
> For we must be his moyles* while he means to bestride us.

These verses probably amused many people in the town, even if they did not admit it openly, and another incident probably aroused even more mirth and gossip. Rosewarne had a poor cousin, Mrs Loveday Incledon, the wife of a St Keverne man who practised as a doctor, probably with little qualification. Mr Rosewarne did not acknowledge this humble relation who went from town to town in the red cloak of a countrywoman selling quack remedies. One day when she was in Truro and he was entertaining "lords, and baronets, and ladies, gay and glistening", her strange figure appeared at the door accompanied by Dr Wolcot

John Wolcot, better known as Peter Pindar: a portrait by his protégé John Opie   (Courtesy RIC)

---

* moyles - mules

who pushed towards the outraged host this mud-bespattered woman with the words, "Henry! your cousin Incledon; Mrs Incledon! your cousin Henry!" Rosewarne was said never to have forgiven Wolcot for this and in the end Wolcot found it expedient to move elsewhere, taking with him the young painter, John Opie, whom he had befriended. In London both found fame: Opie as the "Cornish Wonder", a sought-after society portrait painter, and Wolcot as a political satirist under the name of Peter Pindar. Perhaps there in the capital they met Mrs Incledon's son, Charles, who made his debut at Covent Garden in 1790 and became one of the most famous tenors of his day.

In 1783 Rosewarne died at his new home of Bosvigo on the outskirts of the town. He was succeeded as Vice-Warden of the Stannaries by his friend John Thomas "whose talents and knowledge and integrity as an Attorney-at-law were equalled by few, and as Vice-Warden of the Stannaries by none", according to Richard Polwhele. He inherited the Chiverton estate near the village of Zelah, where he built for himself a grand house with "excellent gardens and flourishing shrubberies and plantations."[35] This was the same John Thomas who, as a boy, had shot Mr Lemon's pet chough.

"A stranger will be very much struck, at his first entrance into Truro, to see the blocks (of tin) that lie in heaps about the streets." So wrote W.G.Maton of his visit in the 1790s.[36] He continued: "Every block is worth ten or twelve guineas, weighing sometimes 320 pounds - a load too great for a thief to carry off without discovery. More tin and copper are exported hence than from any port in the country." This is what marked Truro out from other towns, and both the Lemon and Daniell families continued to reap the benefits from the mining industry. Ralph Allen Daniell, Thomas's son, continued his father's enterprises and added to them a large copper smelting works in Glamorgan. Richard Polwhele, his friend, wrote: "His income from the mines was at one time incredibly great. From the Seal-hole he had an inundation of riches, at the rate of a guinea a minute!" Soon "Guinea-a-minute Daniell" became his nickname. Polwhele added: "His return to the property-tax commissioners was one year so magnificent - I dare not report it."[37]

With this great wealth he added other establishments for his growing household. In 1784 he had married Elizabeth Pooley, daughter of the Vicar of Ladock, and over the following years they had twelve children, six girls and six boys. They kept a house in fashionable Bath as well as in London, and in about 1800 he bought as his country residence Trelissick, a few miles from Truro, which he enlarged and embellished. Here his large family would have gardens, parkland, a beach and the tidal waters of the Fal for their playground. He took a greater part in public life than did his father, being Mayor of Truro in

1792, Sheriff in 1795 and an MP for West Looe in three successive parliaments.
As a child he would have seen changes being made in Truro. The
church at last was given a steeple 125 feet high, which was completed in 1769,
so "the pitiful little thing...looking rather like a pigeon house than a church
tower", as scathingly described in Andrew Brice's Gazetteer ten years earlier,
was replaced by a grander structure, although when it was dismantled nearly
120 years later it was found to have been built on poor foundations and was in
a very shaky condition. Two bells were hung in it, but they were only to be
rung together in case of fire. Before these were in place Atty White, the town
crier, would go through the streets ringing his handbell before a service. The
Corporation then ordered that a "large and handsome clock be erected in the
Tower adjoining the Church". This had four faces so that it could be seen
from all directions - perhaps an indication that time was becoming more
important.

St Mary's church with its new steeple, which was criticised by some
as being out of keeping with the Gothic church
(Nineteenth-century engraving, courtesy Cornish Studies Library)

A few years later the eastern entry into the town was improved by the
building of a second bridge, the New Bridge, where there was a ford a little

lower down the river than the older East Bridge. In the 1790s, when as an adult Ralph Allen Daniell was taking a full part in the life of the town and the county, there were even greater changes being made, partly through the influence of his older contemporary, Sir William Lemon, grandson of the "Great William Lemon", who had been created a baronet in 1774.

The bridge, New Bridge Street

When John Swete, a wealthy Devon clergyman, visited the town in 1780 he had dinner at a "neat inn", the King's Head, "lately built by Sir William Lemon".[38] This was one of the two best hostelries in the town, situated where Lower Lemon Street nowadays joins Boscawen Street. In fact at that time the building was not new but had recently been given a facelift, being repaired and refitted "in an elegant manner."[39] Swete then described the main street on which it stood as "a long contracted mean street." A petition sent by the borough to Parliament complained that the streets in the town were in a ruinous state "that various encroachments are made into them and nuisances suffered to remain therein." Parliamentary assent was granted for "paving, cleansing, lighting and widening the streets, lanes and passages, for removing and preventing encroachments, nuisances and annoyances and for regulating the porters and the drivers of carts within the borough."

In 1797, when John Skinner visited, he reported: "The improvements made in Truro of late years have been considerable... The principal street was formerly contracted, and disfigured by a row of houses, stretching along the middle from the Coinage Hall to the Market place. These have been removed, and a spacious opening formed, from which a new street is now building, diverging from the other at right angles, through which the road proceeds to Falmouth." Truro was being revolutionised.

The destruction of Middle Row opened up a broad area in the centre of the town transforming the two narrow, medieval streets into a wide, airy space, soon to be called Boscawen Street, an acknowledgement that this influential landowning family was still important to the town and that the political furore caused by Rosewarne had just been an unfortunate, temporary upset. Houses on the south side of the street which had fronted the River Kenwyn were now rebuilt with their fronts facing the more impressive main street.[40] There was now more room for the growing number of wheeled vehicles coming into the town, especially for the hurrying wheels of the new Royal Mail coaches, but the steepness of St George's Chapel Hill, the main road out of the town to Redruth, created real problems for the coaches. Various possibilities were discussed for improving this approach and a new street from the centre was decided on, which would have an easier gradient, over land owned by Sir William Lemon. There were two obstacles to overcome: a new bridge over the River Kenwyn would be needed, and a way through into Boscawen Street would have to be made.

The bridge was easily dealt with, but the King's Head blocked off the bottom of the new street and would have to go. (This was the inn where a wainscoted room with an old arched window and carved figures of the apostles possibly indicated the site of the medieval chapel of the Guild of St Nicholas.) Sir William Lemon was ready to build a new inn facing on to the new street, and then demolish the old one. However, his tenant, the innkeeper, had other ideas and refused to move into these premises when they were ready in 1801. The architect and builder in charge of the arrangements, William Wood, finally hit on a plan, which he revealed in a hurried letter to Sir William's lawyer. "I almost despaired of ever getting them out of the old house - at last I formed a resolution and pulled out the kitchen grates on last Wednesday morning and fitted them into the new house - being well assured they would follow the cook - this was done while they were fast asleep - this manoeuvre got them all of a bustle and the goods removed by whole sale and the mason stripping the roof same time."[41] This episode seems to be the only indication of the reaction of the ordinary people of the town to all these changes.

Along the new street plots of land were leased by Sir William for building, and in spite of the piecemeal development that followed, these houses, many built of the local Newham stone which was pale gold in colour like Ralph Allen's Bath stone, created an elegant and attractive street climbing up the hill. It has been described as the best Georgian street west of Bath, and not surprisingly it was given the name "Lemon Street". Sir William was also the MP for the county, which position he held for fifty years, and by the time he died in December 1824 he was known as "the Father of the House."

Nineteenth-century engraving showing Lemon Bridge and Lemon Street
(Courtesy Cornish Studies Library)

Other streets seem to have been renamed around this time, with noble-sounding names: "King Street" leading from High Cross to Boscawen Street, and "Prince's Street" and "Duke Street" on either side of the Duchy Coinage Hall. It was hardly surprising that James Forbes described Truro as "the County Town". A Trade Directory for the 1790s stated: "The people of this town dress and live so elegantly that the *pride* of Truro is one of the bye-words of this county."[42]

Truro was a rich and confident town. These years of the second half of the eighteenth century and the early years of the nineteenth century could be described as Truro's "Golden Age". To it came adventurers and engineers concerned with the finances and technicalities of mining, curious visitors like James Forbes and the others quoted here, and to it also came people looking for enjoyment and entertainment, because Truro was becoming the social centre for a wide area.

*A selection of Truro doorways in eighteenth-
or early nineteenth-century style (Can you identify them?)*

References

[1] Forbes, J., "A Tour into Cornwall to the Land's End, 1794", JRIC 1983
[2] Gibson, A.(ed.), 1968
[3] Palmer, 1990
[4] Barton, 1971
[5] Henderson, J.S., "Notes on the Smelting of Tin at Newham", JRIC 1913
[6] Palmer, 1990 & Douch 1977
[7] Palmer, 1990 & Douch, "Cornish Goldsmiths", JRIC 1970
[8] Barton, 1971 & Douch, ibid.
[9] Palmer, 1990
[10] Truro Buildings Research Group, *Princes Street & the Quay Area*
[11] Douch, 1977
[12] Gibson, A (ed), 1968
[13] Barton, B., *Copper Mining in Devon and Cornwall,* Barton, 1978
[14] Polwhele, 1831
[15] Polwhele, 1803-8 & Palmer, 1990
[16] Rea, J., in *History Around the Fal,* Part V, Fal Local History Group, 1990
[17] Polwhele, 1836
[18] Henderson, Calendar 9
[19] Polwhele, 1803-8
[20] Rea, op.cit.
[21] Hawkridge, C., "Sarah of Trewarthenick", JRIC 1969
[22] Spry, "Notes relating to the Dominican Friary and to St Mary's Church, Truro", Report, RIC 1840 (S)
[23] Jenkin, 1951
[24] Gibson, (ed.), 1968
[25] Spry, op.cit.
[26] Edward, C.,(ed.) "A Visit to Cornwall in 1755", JRIC 1981
[27] Polwhele,1836
[28] Jennings, P., "The Mayoralty of Truro", JRIC XVI
[29] Polwhele, 1831
[30] Polwhele, 1803-8
[31] Polwhele, 1836
[32] Palmer, 1990
[33] Pennington, 1973
[34] Palmer, 1990

[35] Polsue, 1867-73
[36] Gibson (ed.), 1968
[37] Polwhele, 1803-8
[38] Hull, P., "Tours by William Wynne and John Swete", JRIC 1957
[39] Truro Buildings Research Group, *Boscawen Street Area*
[40] Jennings, P., "The Expansion of Truro", JRIC XV
[41] Truro Buildings Research Group, *Lemon Street and its Neighbourhood*
[42] *Universal British Directory*, 1793-8

Chapter 6

A Kaleidoscope of Truro Life

In 1780, the year of the political upset caused by Henry Rosewarne, sleeping inhabitants of Truro were awoken by a group of young people led by Miss Dickenson and Captain Croker dancing cotillions through the streets by the light of the moon. The Mayor, annoyed by this disturbance, sent for the constables and threatened to commit them. This was no rabble-rousing group of people but part of the elite of the town, Elizabeth Dickenson being a great beauty lauded by both Richard Polwhele and Dr Wolcot. Polwhele wrote: "The names of Rosewarne and Dickenson conjure up before me Power and Beauty," and on another occasion he wrote "Miss D. is, at this moment, the animating soul of the place." Wolcot's poem to her, in the classical conventions of the age, refers to Jove who in ancient times was forced to create three women to show the qualities of Love, Virtue and Grace.

But (so improv'd his art divine!)
In one fair female now they shine.

He was a welcome visitor at her parents' house and perhaps had first-hand experience of her calming influence in the household when they had fierce rows, or as Polwhele described it, "the wounds mutually inflicted on each other by her parents, in the bitter domestic skirmish, (which) was always in her power to heal." He also added: "It was in parties of which Wolcot and Miss D. were the enlivening spirits, that I passed many delightful hours."

Her sense of fun obviously coincided with Wolcot's, as shown by one of Polwhele's stories when they teased one of their acquaintances, Miss Giddy, after Wolcot had compared her skill on the pianoforte with Cecilia, the patron saint of music. This reference was lost on Miss Giddy, who believed their assurance that Cecilia was the great grandmother of the harpsichord maker.

Elizabeth Dickenson must have made quite an impression in Truro society because Polwhele also wrote a poem to three beauties which ended with this verse:

Rise Dickenson! - eclipse them both!
Shine out, and carry all before ye!
Venus is happy to make oath -
Thy radiant orb is Truro's glory!

122

A Kaleidoscope of Truro Life

The other two beautiful young women were Miss Coppinger, "the wild girl" who married a Trefusis, and Betsy Cranch, the daughter of the vicar of St Clement, whose "melting charms" caused one man to commit suicide when she refused his advances in favour of John Vivian, whom she married in 1774 while she was still a minor. Wolcot, who must have had an eye for a pretty girl, wrote: "What a fine creature she was! I once told her in jest that she must be my wife, for I had never been so deeply in love before. 'It is out of the question, my dear doctor', she replied; 'it is impossible. I am *five deep* already!'" "In her time," wrote Polwhele, "Truro was 'full of life and splendour and joy', mainly attributable to 'her sweet influence'." He continued, "her benevolence, her affability, her extensive charities, should have left an impression on every mind, deep and infallible."

Her husband, John Vivian, became the most influential man in Truro. He has been called "the founder of the copper trade in Cornwall"[1] becoming the Deputy-Governor of the newly-founded Cornish Metal Company set up in 1785 to try and control the price of copper, when copper deposits in Anglesey were threatening the Cornish industry. Vivian tried hard to persuade some of the adventurers to stop over-producing, but several of the mines lost heavily until the Anglesey deposits were worked out. Matthew Boulton (the business partner of James Watt) recorded one rowdy meeting with the Cornish mine owners and adventurers in Truro where Thomas Williams of the Anglesey Company, "told them in a full meeting that although he never had a great opinion of their wisdom yet he had no idea of their being half so ignorant as he found them."[2] Vivian became Mayor of Truro in 1791, a year before Ralph Allen Daniell, and later Vice-Warden of the Stannaries after the resignation of John Thomas in 1817. According to Polwhele: "Rosewarne had great sway; but John Vivian had greater. In most towns, I believe there is some leader whom the rest of the inhabitants, high and low, follow, as naturally as hounds the most sagacious of the pack. ...This influence is now wearing away. In Truro, I think, it almost expired with John Vivian."

Men like Vivian, who hosted some of the concerts of the Truro Harmonic Society which was formed in the 1790s, Rosewarne with his lavish suppers, the Lemons and the Daniells, provided the high society of Truro with many of their select entertainments. Less refined amusements might also draw the gentry to the town and like the Lemons they might have a town house to use, particularly in the winter when the condition of the roads made travel difficult. Sarah Gregor, of Trewarthenick near Tregony, wrote in her memoirs that any form of entertainment was welcome when neighbours were several miles distant and roads often impassable. She referred to an eighteenth-century entry in the family account book: "expenses when the coach went to Truro taking the young ladies to see the bear." She commented: "A single bear was enough to rouse the squire's family with the mighty effort of driving into Truro; not the trifling effort which now occupies about 50 minutes, but a laborious journey of seven weary miles which four stout horses could scarcely effect in three hours through mud and ruts guiltless of Macadam."[3]

Polwhele remembered these days of his youth as a time when there was "more social intercourse among the people of Truro, than at the present day."

> *My townsmen erst were pleasant folks,*
> *From Keyhead to the Castle;*
> *At every corner cracking jokes!*
> *'Twas one continual wassal.*

> *With no proud gait - no scowling eye,*
> *No sanctified grimaces*
> *From Atty White to Parson Pye*
> *They all had happy faces.*

James Watt obviously did not approve of the light-heartedness of Truro society. When he sent his favourite son, Gregory, to Cornwall in 1797 he instructed his agent not to let him "make any long stay in Truro. Many of the company he would meet there are improper."[4]

Dances, open to a wider selection of people, and the occasional concert and theatrical performance were also held either in the Town Hall over the market or in the Coinage Hall, both ancient buildings not designed for such functions. On one memorable occasion in 1785 royalty attended one of these performances in the Coinage Hall. Young Prince William, later to become King William IV, the Sailor King, after the death of his older brother, George IV, was entertained by Lord Falmouth when his ship, in which he served as a midshipman, arrived in the Fal and moored off Tregothnan. He was taken on a visit to local mines and then to Truro for some light amusement. So many people wanted to attend the performance, perhaps to see the Prince rather than the players, that temporary wooden galleries were erected in the room. Under the crush and weight of people one of the galleries began to creak ominously and threaten a collapse. Once the alarm was over the young visitor laughingly said, "I'll go back and tell George that his old palace is falling about his ears".[5]

Perhaps it was this incident that prompted the building of proper Assembly Rooms, to emulate those in other social centres such as Bath. Truro's

Only the façade of the Assembly Rooms exists today.

Assembly Rooms were unique, being designed for use both as a theatre and for dances. "The theatre...is so judiciously contrived within as to be either perfectly adapted for scenic representations or easily converted into an elegant ball-room, connected with which are card-rooms, and apartments for refreshments."

A Kaleidoscope of Truro Life

So states Heard's *Cornwall Gazetteer* printed in Truro in 1817, thirty years after the building was begun. Gilbert, in his *Survey of Cornwall*, explains how this was achieved: "by laying an additional floor over the pit (it) is converted at the proper time of the year, into an Assembly Room." This classically-designed building with its symmetrical façade, pediment and tall sash windows, was built in the centre of the town in High Cross, close to the church, on the site of what had been the London Inn.[6] Only the façade is now left for us to admire beside the Cathedral, with its plaster medallions of Shakespeare, and David Garrick the famous actor and theatre manager who had died a few years before this building opened.

David Garrick knew Samuel Foote, an actor and playwright from Truro, who had also operated in London in the middle years of the eighteenth century. They were rivals and although they would sometimes dine together, they were not friends. "Whenever they met...Samuel never failed to launch the shafts of his satire against Garrick, who was obliged to sit dumb in his presence."[7] Samuel had been baptised in Truro in 1721, his father being "the old justice" as Polwhele called him, who had a town house as well as a summer residence at Pencalenick. He discovered his enjoyment and ability at acting while he was a pupil at the Grammar School, where he out-shone all the others in the plays of the Roman comedy writer, Terence. This was in the days of George Conon who did not approve of the theatre as a profession and removed these plays from the school curriculum in horror when his old pupil appeared on the London stage for the first time. In the capital his satirical plays and his own comic performances soon became famous. Samuel's flamboyant visits to his old school were dreaded by Conon, according to Richard Polwhele, who remembered one such visit when the actor stumped into the school on his artificial leg (a bad hunting accident had led to amputation above the knee) and without any conferring with the master had laughingly dismissed the boys for a holiday with no work.

Although he inherited money as well as earning more from successful plays, he could not manage it sensibly, a failing he perhaps inherited from his mother, "a lady of considerable vivacity".[8] On one occasion she wrote a hurried note to him:

> *Dear Sam,*
> *I am in prison for debt: come and assist*
> *Your loving mother,*
> *E. Foote.*

His reply stated simply:

Dear Mother,
So am I: which prevents his duty being
paid to his loving mother by
Her affectionate son,
Sam Foote.

Happily for her he added this postscript:

I have sent my attorney to assist you: in the
meantime let us hope for better days.

His plays are not now known: the satirical attacks on people and society of his day have not stood the test of time. Nor do the titles of the plays, performed in the new Assembly Rooms in October 1789, mean much to us nowadays: *The Grecian Daughter, Catherine and Peter the Great,* and a farce called *The Romp.* These were part of a grand gala week, possibly marking the official opening of the rooms.

To Truro for this occasion came the famous Sarah Siddons, who was at this time "the unquestioned queen of the stage" in London.[9] Her clear diction obviously made a big impression on the church organist, Charles Bennet, because this was mentioned fifteen years later in his obituary; his sense of hearing being particularly important to help compensate for his blindness. No doubt the inns and streets of Truro were buzzing with activity and the town houses of the gentry were full as people flocked into the town for this exciting occasion, while carriages and sedan chairs conveyed gorgeously attired men and women shimmering in silks, glittering with jewels, sitting erect under their curled and powdered wigs, to and from the Theatre.

In the following years Assemblies were regularly held here during the winter months. The presence of army officers stationed in the town added colour and excitement to these occasions because without them the young ladies often found a lamentable lack of men to dance and flirt with, so they were prepared to endure a long and uncomfortable ride to enjoy these opportunities. In February 1805 John Whitaker, the rector of Ruan

TRURO ASSEMBLY

THE next TRURO ASSEMBLY will be on THURSDAY the 3d of November.

October 27, 1814

Lanihorne, wrote to Richard Polwhele: "On Thursday my wife and daughters mean to be at Truro, in order to attend the last assembly for the winter, to reach Truro about eight in the evening and return home about three in the morning."

Theatrical performances were less frequent and the standard of the London players could not easily be matched. In 1807 a theatre season organised by a Falmouth manager was a failure, the Shakespeare plays gaining little support, with only the novelty acts and comic songs winning some praise. The *Royal Cornwall Gazette* concluded that this failure of Truro audiences was because: "The high order of its inhabitants, enjoying the advantages of a good education, and being in the habit of frequenting London and Bath, have too highly refined their taste for dramatic performances to relish the fare of a provincial theatre."

Truro was too far away from the metropolis to have regular visits from famous performers, but a few months earlier, in September 1806, another glittering occasion had been arranged: the first Truro Music Festival, with professional instrumentalists and singers, including the soprano Mrs Dickons, a firm favourite, coming from London. Performances included three concerts in the church, with Handel's *Messiah* drawing in the crowds, and three evening concerts in the Theatre with a variety of "Symphonies, Songs, Solos, and Concertos." "All the world is to be here: every room in the town will be crowded, and 'three in a bed' will be deemed comfortable lodging," reported the *Royal Cornwall Gazettte*.[10] A letter printed later confirmed this, describing the roads to the town filled with "country psalm-singers", "blind fiddlers" and "carriages...among which were some very handsome coaches and four with coronets". This was a great success, the paper reporting: "To sum up the whole, the selection, the performance, and the support which the managers have received from the stewards and the public, have so satisfied all parties that it has been proposed and unanimously carried and accepted, to renew this festival triennially." Two more of these festivals were arranged, although the first of these did not have the pull of famous soloists and was less well-attended. In the meantime Truro people had a chance to hear the highly-lauded tenor, Charles Incledon, who made his first professional appearance in his home county in 1808, where he displayed both "tenderness" and "heroic energy" in his repertoire of arias, songs and ballads.[11]

Fifty years earlier there would have been little chance of London players and musicians travelling the long and difficult route to Cornwall. Even in 1806 the first music festival very nearly did not take place as planned because the musicians were late arriving, as the boat they were sailing in from Plymouth was forced in to Fowey by bad weather.[12] Sarah Gregor wrote in her memoirs: "In my youth Cornish roads were proverbially the worst in England and the county was rarely visited by strangers." She also wrote: "A coach might reach London in ten days but the journey was so hazardous that people settled their affairs before they left."[13] A petition to Parliament in 1754 stated that the roads radiating from Truro "are become very ruinous and many places whereof are so narrow that carriages cannot pass each other, and many parts especially in winter and rainy seasons are so deep and founderous that wheeled carriages, horses laden and even travellers, pass in great danger."[14] But this was to change and Polwhele showed the huge improvements that came about during these years. "It was not more than fifty years ago that our first gentry resigned the saddle for the more luxurious chaise or coach. We have now coaches scarcely to be enumerated from London to the Lands End. There is one (if not more) which travel from London to Falmouth in 41 hours."

William Lemon's post chaise must have been one of the first in the county, but one man's memories, published later in the *West Briton*, tell of another coach. "In my early days there were few carriages. ...I saw the first gentleman's carriage ever brought into Cornwall. It was kept at St Erth and belonged to Sir Christopher Hawkins. His men had to pull down the hedges to get it home because of the narrow roads."[15] This was the Trewinnard Coach, which can be seen today in the Royal Cornwall Museum.

The increase in wheeled vehicles in Cornwall was only made possible by improvements to the roads which began around Truro with the formation of

The Trewinnard Coach before restoration

TRURO TURNPIKE.

NOTICE IS HEREBY GIVEN, that the Tolls arising at the several Toll Gates here undermentioned will be LET by AUCTION, to the best Bidder, at the Town-Hall, in the Borough of Truro, on Tuesday the 14th of June next, between the hours of Eleven and Two, in the manner directed by an Act passed in the thirteenth year of the reign of His present Majesty, for regulating the Turnpike Roads, which Tolls the last year Let at the undermentioned sums, and will be put up at the same;

Short Lane's End Gate - - - £ 96	0	
Mitchell Road Gates - - - - 227	0	
Redruth Road Gates - - - - 312	0	
Redruth Gate - - - - - - 115	0	
Penryn Road Gates - - - 181	10	
Grampond Road Gates - - - 317	0	
Penryn Gates - - - - 102	0	
Carnon Gate - - - - - 50	0	

Whoever happens to be the best Bidder, must at the same time give security, with sufficient sureties, to the satisfaction of the Trustees of the said Turnpike Road, for payment of the Rent agreed for, and at such times as they shall direct.

N. B. No Gate Keeper will be permitted to bid for his Gate again, that is any part of May month in arrears. JOHN HENWOOD,

Clerk to the Trustees.

Dated Truro, May 25, 1814.

the Truro Turnpike Company in 1754. By 1795 a traveller by coach described the Falmouth road as "excellent all the way", and the one to Grampound as "good road over many hills."[16] One intrepid man who made the long, hard journey to Cornwall thirty-two times to bring hope and encouragement to poor, hard-living miners and fishermen, was John Wesley. His early journeys were always on horseback, but as he aged and roads improved he was able to travel by chaise. In 1781, when he was in his late seventies, he wrote in his journal: "Between nine and ten we had such a storm of rain as I do not remember to have seen in Europe before. It seemed ready to beat in the windows of the chaise, and in three minutes drenched our horsemen from head to foot. We reached Truro however, at the appointed time."

Among the first regular users of the improved roads were Russell's wagons: heavy, lumbering vehicles drawn by four horses never going faster than walking pace. They must have become a familiar sight in Truro as they passed through once a week (becoming more frequent later) on their way from London to Falmouth and back, often accompanied by other travellers willing to walk beside them during the day and sleep under their cover by night for the protection they provided. The route to and from the packet port of Falmouth was vital, because not only were important messages delivered and sent out from there, but treasure was also regularly landed and transported on Russell's wagons to the capital. On these occasions they would have trundled through Truro accompanied by four soldiers marching to the side and rear as well as having the driver and guard armed with blunderbuss and horse pistols.[17]

These were in marked contrast to the pounding hooves and spinning wheels of the Royal Mail coaches which began to replace the slow and unreliable postboys on horseback from 1784, the first reference to them in Cornwall being in the 1790s, when the post arrived at Truro at seven in the evening and was sent off at seven in the morning.[18] What a splendid sight these coaches must have been, giving way to no-one, the turnpikes flung open wide for the galloping horses as the guard's horn heralded their headlong approach! One man's memory of them in Truro was published in the *Royal Cornwall Gazette*. "And then the Royal Mail Coach coming down Lemon Street, the proud coachman, the gold-laced coat of the guard, his silver horn, his blunderbuss, the hasty move of the passengers, changing the horses."[19]

In 1799 an advertisement gave details of mail coach journeys between Exeter and Falmouth, the journey to be completed during one long day, starting from Exeter at one in the morning and not arriving in Falmouth until the evening. The cost for the passengers, who would not have had a comfortable ride, was £2 10s each for the four passengers who sat inside, while another four could brave the elements sitting outside for £1 11s 4d each. Fifty years later the Royal Quicksilver Mail was advertising this journey as lasting only ten hours with the fares reduced to £1 15s inside and £1 3s outside.

These coaches were used only on the main roads, and places off these routes would still depend on slow and less secure methods. In 1804 a man was sent to Bodmin gaol for attempting to rob the postboy carrying the mail from Truro to Lord Falmouth's estate at Tregothnan. The direct way there was to cross the river by ferry at Malpas (pronounced *Mopus*), which is where the

Photograph (taken probably early this century)
courtesy Royal Cornwall Polytechnic Society

attempt was made. It failed, not so much because of the postboy's defence but because the ferry was rowed by the "Great Jenny" (pictured opposite), a woman of tremendous strength, and it was her fists and flailing arms that foiled the robbery. On another occasion when she was asked what caused her the most trouble on the ferry, her answer was succinct: "Wemmen and pigs."

Cheap and Expeditious

TRAVELLING

From TRURO to REDRUTH, CAMBORNE, FRADDON, MARAZION, and PENZANCE.

THE Public are most respectfully informed, that an elegant Light

POST COACH, -

Carrying Four Inside and Ten Outside Passengers,

CALLED THE

ROYAL DISPATCH,

Will begin on Monday the 18th Instant,

TO RUN FROM

TRURO to PENZANCE,

Mondays, Wednesdays, and Fridays, and return Tuesdays, Thursdays and Saturdays, and to carry Passengers at 10s. Inside, and 7s. Outside, and shorter Stages in proportion.

It stops at the following Places ;

Pearce's Hotel, - - - -	*Truro.*
Pearce's Hotel, - - - -	*Redruth.*
Knapp's, Prince George, -	*Camborne.*
Star, - - - - - - -	*Marazion.*
Reeves's Hotel - - - - -	*Penzance.*

As the main roads improved travellers had greater choice of modes of transport with the competition provided by the stage coaches. In 1799 a stage coach was advertised as running between Torpoint and Truro twice a week each way, stopping overnight in Truro at the Queen's Head. This was an inn close to the West Bridge, the main entry into the town from Falmouth until the new route down Lemon Street was opened. With the new road the King's Head, soon to change its name to Pearce's Hotel, was very conveniently placed to cater for the growing demand, particularly as it had plenty of stabling for the large number of horses that were needed. A few yards away, in Boscawen Street, stood the Red Lion, also well-placed for coaches. Even before the advent of many stage coaches the Red Lion was advertising in 1769 its superior accommodation, having just moved along the street to Mr Foote's Great House "fitted up...in a very genteel manner." The landlord, Mr Gatty, stated that "The House is by far the best in Cornwall" and he had laid in the "best provisions and wines of every kind."

"Jenny Mopus" (Courtesy RIC)

133

Thirty-six years later the reputation of the Red Lion was still being maintained. William Jenkin, agent to the Agar-Robartes family, wrote: "The Red Lyon in Truro is undoubtedly the best Inn there," but he then added, "The King's Head is a tolerable good house and is patronised by Sir William Lemon and many other respectable characters."[20] By this time the growing number of mail and stage coaches, as well as private carriages, ensured that these two hostelries became the main coaching inns for the town.

The famous oak staircase at the Red Lion. Since the demolition of the building in 1967, the staircase has been in pieces at Godolphin House. (Photograph courtesy Clive Benney)

As well as accommodating visitors, these inns could also provide private rooms for business meetings and cater for various dinners and other functions held by the townspeople, and it was in one of these two inns that old boys of the Grammar School would gather for the annual School Meeting, which was like an Old Boys' Reunion. They would first meet for a service in the church, almost next door to the school, and then some of the current pupils would perform, not musical or theatrical entertainments as might happen today, but declamations in prose or verse in both English and Latin, because their education was based on the classic writers.[21]

The Old Grammar School in St Mary's Street

Once the formal part was over the men would dine at one of the inns where no doubt many a memory of their schooldays would be recalled: the times they were rapped over the knuckles or flogged for not preparing their work or for failing to transpose Sapphic odes into hexameter verse; or the pranks they got up to out of the classroom. They might remember the time when one of their number had dared to complain about the breakfast broth which was heated up from the previous day. The punishment from Mr Conon was a hit on his hand so hard that the boy's thumb had been put out of joint. They might talk of the times when, as Richard Polwhele relates, they fought with the town boys in the streets and on the Green, or lay in wait outside the bakehouse to seize the pies as they came hot from the oven, or swung on the school bell-rope to plaster the face of Minerva, which decorated the ceiling, with mud from their boots. They might recount the horrific discovery made by some boys, who rushed from their lessons when a shot rang out nearby, to find Dr Hopson lying on the floor of his house "weltering in his own blood", having killed himself in despair when Betsy Cranch refused his advances.[22]

When the names of old boys were raised no doubt the name of Ned Pellew was often mentioned: the time he sprang over the high back gate of the Red Lion to help put out a fire, the times when he played truant and could be found on the quay amongst the boats, and the time when his fiery temper got him into the last of his fights with school mates when, after injuring one boy, he ran away before he could be punished. He left behind him memories and, like many another boy before and since, his name carved into the desks, "a great because a forbidden pleasure."[23] He soon joined the navy, when he was still only thirteen years old, and took part in some of the actions of the American War of Independence. Truro people would have little trouble in recalling the time after this war, when Captain Edward Pellew returned to Truro, became a member of the Corporation and took a part in the political machinations of the 1780s. On one occasion in 1784, he challenged one of the Whigs on the council to a duel and came armed to a meeting, which caused a furore.[24] His later exploits in the wars against France would again, no doubt, become the subject of animated discussions.

Cornish mining was going through difficult times towards the end of the century, partly because of the discovery of easily-obtained copper deposits in Anglesey, and the mine managers were irked by the need to pay James Watt and his business partner, Matthew Boulton, for the use of Watt's steam pumping engines. Much of the talk at Reunions during these years must have been on these difficulties because many of the gentlemen would have had financial interests in mining. There would have been much speculation when in 1781 another old boy, Jonathan Hornblower, patented his invention of a double-cylinder engine, which he hoped would overcome the Watt monopoly. Maybe some of these men were in the King's Head one day in early September 1786 and witnessed the strange sight of William Murdoch's small steam carriage puffing its way around "Mr River's great room" carrying a fire shovel, poker and tongs, the first public demonstration of this invention by Boulton and Watt's engineer.[25] Would they have dismissed this as just a toy or seriously discussed the possible significance of this form of transport for the future?

In more light-hearted vein Richard Polwhele might have recounted some of the other stories he was later to write about. The time when he and three friends were on the hill above the Truro river when they saw on the far side at

Newham, Charles Bennet, the blind organist of
St Mary's, going bird-nesting with the boy
who acted as his guide. The boys shouted
across to him, not dreaming that he would
be able to hear the words they were
using at that distance, only to find that
the headmaster, Cornelius Cardew,
kept them in school, following a bitter
complaint from the organist. Or he
might recall the time when one of his
friends played a joke on him when
drilling like soldiers was all the rage
amongst the boys. Polwhele as
"Colonel" of the troop was to lead his
"men" in military manoeuvres to perform
in front of the girls at the boarding school
of Tregolls. Polwhele sensibly arranged
for a professional soldier in Truro to carry

Richard Polwhele

out the drill,only to find to his dismay that his friend had bribed the man to stay
away.

The girls' education would bear little comparison with the classical
learning of these boys. Sarah Gregor, who attended a fashionable London
boarding school in the early years of the nineteenth century, described what
was expected of them. "A girl needed only a very small amount of knowledge
to be accused of being a blue-stocking; if she could read and write and spell
and had a sketchy knowledge of geography and arithmetic, she was 'well-
informed'; if she could play a sonata or two and could do a polished curtsey,
she was 'exceptionally accomplished'."[26] Some French was learned only
because of the huge number of French refugees who poured acrosss the Channel
to escape the guillotine or worse, and were prepared to teach for little pay.
Dancing and deportment were important subjects. "We learnt to enter a room,
to leave it, to step into a carriage and to curtsey, to be graceful if Nature
permitted it, at the expense of much time and torture." The "torture" was
explained by chairs "in which with feet in stocks and head in harness attached
to a pole we sat, screwed up to the length of throat required by the rules of
proportion laid down by authority." If this discomfort were not enough their
living conditions gave them little relief. The one fire was monopolised by the
teachers, washing was done in cold water, and food consisted of bread, butter

and cold mutton, followed by rice pudding "full of unpleasant black things which were believed to be the corpses of animals who had endeavoured to fore-stall us as rice-eaters".

There is no way of knowing if the boarding school at Tregolls was as bad as this, but according to Polwhele it was started on the plan of a London boarding school some time in the middle part of the eighteenth century by Miss Mitchell, "a sensible and well-informed lady" who was the daughter of the Vicar of Veryan. She had first opened the school in the Great House by the Green where both Henry Rosewarne and Richard Polwhele were later to live. Polwhele recalled that his large bedchamber there had been "a dancing room for the ladies of the boarding school." She had then moved the school into a large brick house on the site of what is now the City Hall, and then to Tregolls, on the outskirts of the town. But in spite of her efforts the school was not very successful, Polwhele's explanation being that she "aimed too high for the country." What most people expected at this time of the ladies of high society was not intellectual accomplishments but to be gracious hostesses.

Sarah Gregor's reference to "blue stockings" comes from an attempt by a group of men and women in London to find a more satisfying way of spending their time than the interminable games of cards that were so popular in the eighteenth century. (In Truro there was a Whist Club which met weekly on Monday evenings, and it was said that people arranged their card parties "even at the church door".) This London group met for intellectual conversation and discussion in which eminent men of letters often took part. They included the wife of Admiral Boscawen, the son of the first Viscount Falmouth, who was famous for his naval victories and was for a time in the 1740s and 1750s a popular MP for Truro, nicknamed "Old Dreadnought". It was he who jokingly gave them their name, the Blue Stocking Society, after the colour of the stockings of one of the men in the group, several of whom did not wear the black silk stockings normally worn for formal evening dress. The name "blue stocking" was later used in a derogatory sense, particularly as a criticism of intellectual women.

A wider choice of reading became available in Truro for those able to pay the annual subscription of not less than one guinea, when a library was opened in Prince's Street in 1792. A meeting, chaired by Sir William Lemon, had been held at the Red Lion to discuss the possibility of establishing a "Publick County Library" and Truro was decided as "the most central and advantageous situation for its establishment."[27] Heard's *Cornwall Gazetteer*, published in 1817, stated that it contained about 3,000 books and was managed by a librarian who lived in rooms in the same building, was paid £15 a year and "was removable at pleasure".

Although it was to be many years before girls began to gain equal educational status with boys, Truro in the early years of the nineteenth century seems to have been surprisingly well-supplied with schools, even if the subject matter taught was very restricted. The Town Council supported a writing school housed in the Market Hall until it was pulled down in 1807, and in 1812 a National School opened using Dr Bell's monitorial system of teaching, with older children passing on the knowledge they were taught to the younger ones. This schooling was free for children of the poor, and for those who could afford it, four shillings was charged four times a year for reading, with an extra three shillings a quarter for writing and arithmetic. This school was soon extended to include girls in a separate class with the emphasis for them on arithmetic, especially the ability to add up tradesmen's bills, and sewing, the girls doing work sent in from people in the town who paid the school for this service. In 1817 there were 130 boys and about 70 girls taking advantage of this opportunity. In addition there were a number of private schools, some very small, for both boys and girls. It was in one of these in Coombes Lane that young Richard Lander, the explorer of the River Niger, became a favourite of the master, "old Pascoe", who awarded him one of the newly-coined 1s.6d pieces for his good work.

This emphasis on some school education for poorer children was quite new and not approved of by everyone. Richard Polwhele wrote *Bedlam Broke Loose*, which started:

> *Behold from the Bell school or Bedlam,*
> *(Each urchin fat as any fed lamb)*
> *The insulting tribe play, prank on prank,*
> *And grinning at old age or rank,*
> *Hurl pebbles round, and smash out windows; ...*

In spite of this increase in schools there must have been many children in the town who still had no schooling at all, but there was a growing realisation that new skills were needed in this increasingly industrial age that put Cornwall in the forefront of many other parts of the country. The early years of the nineteenth century, for example, saw a Cornishman, Richard Trevithick the pioneer of high pressure steam power, experiment with steam road engines and put the first steam engine on to rails, which was to give George Stephenson *his* first sight of a steam locomotive. With revolutionary changes like these taking place the supporters of the traditional teaching of the Grammar School were in for a rude shock.

In 1805 the *Royal Cornwall Gazette* advertised a change in the syllabus. In addition to the usual Latin, Greek, Roman Antiquities and Ancient Geography, new subjects were being offered, including Writing, Arithmetic, English Grammar, Modern Geography and the Elements of Natural and Experimental Philosophy, the name then for science. This was the idea of the new headmaster, Thomas Hogg, foreseeing the need for a more liberal education in a changing world. Not everyone approved, feeling that he was lowering the tone of a school that had established for itself a high academic reputation. Perhaps it was with the Cornish "fire engines" (steam-powered beam engines) and Trevithick's "puffing devil" in mind that he advertised the first of a series of lectures, open to all for a payment, except to "the young gentlemen of the school" who could go free, on "Fire and its Properties."[28]

One past pupil who might well have approved of this change was Humphry Davy, who had been at the school for a year in 1792, when he was fourteen years old. Although he had shown himself proficient at translating from the classics into English verse, he wrote to his mother that learning in school was not usually a pleasure.[29] He seemed to get most enjoyment from fishing, shooting or making fireworks.[30] By the time the new courses were being advertised he had already been elected a Fellow of the Royal Society and was drawing appreciative audiences to his lectures and experiments in chemistry at the Royal Institution in London.

Some years later, in 1818, a meeting was held in the Library, chaired by John Vivian, which resolved to form a society for the advancement of Science, to be called the "Cornwall Philosophical Institution". Edward Pellew, by then a Viscount, and a war-hero, accepted the office of President, which he held for the next twelve years. In 1821 Truro's other chief war-hero, General Sir Richard Hussey Vivian, used his influence with the new King, George IV, to gain for it royal patronage and the name of the Royal Institution of Cornwall, which name it still holds. Even at that time it had a small museum, which was to be open every day from 10am until sunset, except on Sundays, and it was prepared to analyse mineral specimens providing that the "mine or person sending the specimen deposit one of a similar nature in the museum." This was the start of the Royal Cornwall Museum, now a historical and geological treasure house, active in education and preservation.

Many of the details in these chapters concern only the minority of people at the top of Truro society. The vast majority have left little to help us gain much insight into their lives. Richard Polwhele, who was for many years curate at Kenwyn church, wrote about one of his predecessors, Parson Karkeek, whose sense of humour back-fired on him on one occasion, when he mimicked, not for the first time, the stuttering talk of one of his parishioners, Crety Hooper, on meeting her one day. She was not amused and flung in his face the contents of the pitcher of milk that she was carrying angrily exclaiming, "Thee were a rook before; I've now made thee a maggoty-pie!". She was a mantua maker in the town, at a time when this form of head-dress was just becoming popular, because she was the only one then, but Polwhele adds "we have now I suppose full 100."

One of these businesses in the early nineteenth century was Mrs Reed's who advertised herself as "Mantua, Pelisse and Dressmaker". She was anxious to tell her prospective clients that her elder daughter had just returned to Truro "with a complete knowledge of whatever is elegant and graceful in female attire," as she had been placed with one of the "first dressmakers of the Court and fashionable circles."[31] Mrs Reed may have been competing for custom with travelling London tailors who found it worthwhile journeying to Cornwall for business, as Polwhele wrote about thirty years later: "It is remarkable, that gowns and other articles of female dress were formerly made by tailors". London fashions changed drastically especially during the 1790s and in the early 1800s, and Mrs Reed was quick to reassure her customers of her up-to-date knowledge. Wide dresses for the ladies and knee breeches for the men were discarded in the later 1790s in favour of the classical simplicity of the new ideas coming in from Revolutionary France. Slim, high-waisted dresses, often of white or pale muslin, were soon *de rigueur* for any young lady of fashion, while the men took to wearing pale skin-tight pantaloons and cut-away coats.

With the change in dress came a corresponding change in hairstyles. One long-standing hairdressing business in Truro was that of the Knuckey family which, over one hundred years later in 1912, was described as being "the oldest of its class in the west of England and perhaps in the whole country". It "had the support of the best families not only near Truro, but throughout the county."[32] In the eighteenth century it was centrally placed, first in High Cross on the site of what became the Assembly Rooms and then moving to King Street. No doubt the Knuckeys and their assistants could be seen hurrying to the grand houses before Assemblies and other social events, armed with combs and other tools of their trade. In the 1780s these would have included powder, grey or white for the gentlemen, and perhaps grey, blue, blonde or brown for the ladies, possibly finished off with a frosting of white. This was the time of wigs for both men and women which could reach fantastic heights and widths.

KNUCKEY AND SONS,
HAIR CUTTERS, WIG MAKERS, HAIR DRESSERS, PERFUMERS, &c.,
BOSCAWEN STREET, TRURO,

RESPECTFULLY announce to their Friends and the Public in general, that W. KNUCKEY has recently returned from London, where he has availed himself of the opportunity of becoming thoroughly acquainted with the most recent Fashions and the latest improvements in every branch of the trade. In the manufacture of Ornamental Hair of every description they have been very successful in producing that ease and gracefulness which are the great desideratum of art. They beg to call attention to their recent improvements in Gentlemen's Perukes, and Ladies' Patent Head Dresses, which are unparallelled for lightness and beauty of workmanship, and are made entirely of natural curled hair. They beg to state that their Establishment is now replete with every description of Fancy Articles, Perfumery, Brushes and Combs, Jewellery, Cutlery, Cricket Bats and Balls, Fishing Rods and Tackle, genuine Naples Soap, and Turkey Sponge.

Knuckey and Sons having made Hair Cutting upon novel and scientific principles their most earnest study, beg to assure those persons who are apt to consider that nature has been most ungenerous to them, that the most untoward head of hair may be rendered graceful, and so arranged as to agree with the contour of the features, as well as with the general expression of the countenance, and that in nine cases out of ten, the inelegant and outre appearance of the hair may with justice be attributed to the unskilful management of the operator.

Boscawen Street, Truro, June 23, 1852.

In the 1790s these began to go out of fashion, as did powder after a tax was put on it. Copying Greek and Roman statues, fashionable men had their hair cut short at back and sides with curls clustering on their forehead. Women also had curls framing their faces with long hair pulled back in a chignon bound round by a filet. The Knuckey family would need to keep up with these changes to attract their best customers. Their job might well be rather unpleasant because even in the 1820s a popular book was stating that hair should never be washed. This was described as "a pernicious practice that could cause head aches, ear aches, tooth aches and complaints of the eyes". It was however allowable to clean the hair with ivory powder or hair bran.[33]

Other tradesmen in Truro must also have earned their living by supplying the needs of the wealthy elite and those who emulated them, such as the two jewellers and the perfumer recorded in the 1790s, and the seller of glass and Staffordshire ware whose goods were beginning to replace the traditional pewter, much to the alarm of some of the tin miners who feared for their livelihoods. Carts carrying this earthenware into Cornwall were often protected by armed guards.

The richer people were making their homes more comfortable with upholstered furniture and carpets on the floor. Truro had one upholsterer in the 1790s and also a carpet factory capable of producing, according to Polwhele, one thousand yards of Brussell's carpeting a week "equal if not superior in quality and colours to any manufactured in the kingdom". In Polwhele's bulky seven-volume *History of Cornwall* he devoted less than half a page to manufactures, mostly about this factory, which was started about 1791. He recorded that between five and seven hundred people were employed in this enterprise, but a visitor to the town in 1795 wrote that seventy were working there, women and girls weaving the inferior carpets, who were kept apart from the men and boys weaving the "Carpets with large flowers." This discrepancy in numbers could be explained, either by a printing error, or because some of the work was done elsewhere. Polwhele wrote that they prepared the wool from "sheep's back through every process until its manufacture" so some of these people may have been living outside the town, not only the farmers but also some spinners and weavers working in their own homes.

During these years and in spite of these changes the life of the town would still have followed the familiar patterns of two or three hundred years earlier. Long lines of pack animals would still be seen bringing tin for the now-quarterly coinages as well as for smelting, but their numbers and frequency would be increasing as production rose, not only of tin but also of copper. Mules as well as horses were now being used and Truro's Town Quay, as well as those along the Kenwyn and the Allen Rivers, could be bustling with activity as these animal trains arrived to deposit yet another load of copper ore and be loaded with yet more coal to feed the ever-hungry steam engines pumping out millions of gallons of water an hour from the mines. The *Royal Cornwall Gazette*'s weekly records of shipping movements show the importance of the trade with Wales. For example for 10 July 1801, of the nine boats that left Truro, eight were sailing with copper for the smelting houses of South Wales and of the fifteen boats that arrived that same week, thirteen were from Wales with their cargoes of coal.

An increasing burden was being put on the pack animals trudging along minor roads not improved by the turnpike system. William Jenkin wrote in December 1799: "The roads are so very bad both to Newham, Pill and Point, that it is little short of cruelty to drive horses and mules over them so frequently as they are at this time of the year. Many accidents thereby happen - it would be better to let the poor creatures rest 2 or 3 days a week."[34] Six years later he referred again to this problem: "There is more ore raising than the Horses can now carry - great numbers of them are very weak, and the Roads excessive

bad." A year later a solution to this problem seemed imminent. "The Eastern Mines are to have canals cut to the several shipping places betwixt Truro and Falmouth and are to be set about quickly." This never happened, but the problem was soon to be resolved by building mineral railways followed by a revolution in transport that was to bring huge changes to Cornwall.

Ships from Norway also arrived loaded with timber for the mines, and timber ponds began to develop along the riverside. Local farmers would also sell their timber, not just for the wood but for the bark which was in great demand by the tanners of Truro. Tanning was still carried on behind Pydar Street, the Ferris family being particularly active in this, and the site of the old friary was used for tanpits.[35] Farmers from some distance away found it profitable to supply them. George Wilce, a farmer in the parish of St Kew, recorded in the 1790s receiving £6 for his "tops of timber", but bark sold in Truro fetched over £34.[36]

Tanyard Court, off Pydar Street

Opposite: Vessels moored at the Town Quay.
Nineteenth-century engraving, courtesy RIC

A Kaleidoscope of Truro Life

Market days still brought farmers and their wives into the town, with the Saturday market having meat, poultry, fish and vegetables on sale. Andrew Brice's unpleasant description of the meat market in 1759 was probably still true at the end of the century. "Though the market-house be a good one, yet 'tis odd that the flesh-meat there should so hang dangling on an end by very long iron crooks, down to one's shoulders; so that persons who come to buy, have a difficulty to escape with their vesture unsmeered with grease and blood." Out in the street the country girls stood with their baskets of geese, poultry and butter in front of them "all rank and file, like a company of soldiers under arms to be reviewed." In 1795 a traveller described the ingenious construction of the market stalls which were on rollers and could be folded up and rolled away for storage between one market day and the next.[37] Not all the traders dealt honestly with their customers. A letter to Richard Polwhele in 1802 referred to a meeting of the magistrates in Truro, when a great number of tradesmen were fined "for deficiency in weights and measures."[38]

The cramped conditions in this old market house could not cope with the increasing population of the town and it had been intended to demolish this building when the rest of Middle Row was knocked down, but there was not enough money at that time to replace it. About thirteen years later plans were once more taking shape. William Jenkin wrote in February 1807: "The Corporation of Truro are very desirous of getting the Seven Stars premises on some terms or other, for the purpose of building a Market House on the spot, which would greatly beautify the Town, and by pulling down the present Market House and Town Hall would remove a great nuisance and eye sore."[39]

These particular negotiations for a site on the north side of Boscawen Street fell through but a site on the south side was then chosen. Sir William Lemon was quick to see the advantages for him, it being close to quays and properties that he owned, and he offered £200 towards the purchase of the land. This time the plans were carried through, but not with complete satisfaction. Heard's Gazetteer in 1817 stated: "The market...is compact and convenient although rather small for the increasing population of the town." It was to serve the town for nearly forty years.

The townspeople could still enjoy the excitement of Fairs four times a year, but the November Fair held in High Cross since medieval times must have been causing problems. In the eighteenth century it was known as the

---

Opposite: Boscawen Street, 1831: the Market gates are just visible on the left and the Red Lion is in the middle of the row on the right.

146

Bullock and Beast Fair and perhaps people were less prepared to put up with the inconveniences of herds of milling cattle blocking up the streets, frisking around or worse, stampeding, to the danger of people nearby. There was an attempt to relocate this fair to the site of the old castle, but it did not last for long. In 1771 an advertisement appeared clearly stating that this was done without the knowledge of the High Lord of the Borough of Truro and that the fair "will in all future times...be held and kept within the said Cross and not elsewhere."

Occasions like these would be a welcome break in the humdrum routine of daily life for many of the nearby villagers as well as for the townspeople, who would expect novelties and entertainments in addition to the serious business of buying and selling. Inns no doubt did brisk trade and alcohol and drunkenness were prevalent at this time, Truro, presumably, being no better or worse than elsewhere. Certainly spirits might be obtained quite cheaply with smuggling rife around the coasts. In the 1790s Truro had two customs and two excise officers but there were too few to keep a watch on all the lonely coves or river landing places. Polwhele tells of a smuggler chased by an excise officer down the steep hill leading to King Harry Ferry, not far from Truro. The smuggler urged his tired horse into the deep waters, then as the horse started to falter under its load, he slid off its back, cut the slings holding the two precious barrels of brandy and then tried desperately, but vainly, to keep the animal's head above water. The horse drowned but the smuggler made it safely to the other side. The *Royal Cornwall Gazette*, in its report on the incident, concluded: "The less mettlesome excise man had halted on the shore, where he surveyed the ineffectual struggle, and afterwards, with the help of the ferryman, got possession of the ankers."

The violent game of hurling was popular, especially in the earlier part of the eighteenth century, the silver ball being thrown up for matches between the men of Truro and their neighbours of Kea or Kenwyn, with the Truro men usually losing the fight into which it could degenerate. Bull baiting and cock fighting were also popular then. Richard Taunton, a Truro doctor in the early nineteenth century, recorded the memories of an old man who could remember the bull being kept on the castle field and brought down Pydar Street to High Cross. There, he said, it duly lowered its head to be tethered to the base of the cross, that was all that was left of this medieval relic, before the dogs were set on it.[40] Gambling would have added to the excitement for the cheering onlookers, as with cock fighting, but during the years when Samuel Walker was curate of St Mary's church his charismatic preaching was said to have drawn people into the church and away from the the playhouse and cockpit. After his death his followers broke away from the Anglican church and for a time used the old round cockpit behind Pydar Street as their base, provoking some of their opponents to mock them in the streets clucking and waving their arms around like hens.

During Samuel Walker's evangelical ministry John Wesley did not feel the need to preach in Truro. Some of Walker's followers were not sympathetic with Wesley who wrote in 1766: "I was in hopes, when Samuel Walker died, the enmity in those who were called his people would have died also. But it is not so; they still look upon us as rank heretics." Wesley's early visits to Cornwall in the 1740s had produced violent opposition in some places partly because his influence over the people was feared by the authorities at a time when the Hanoverian throne seemed under threat from the claims of the Stuart, Bonnie Prince Charlie. With the Prince's defeat at Culloden in 1746 much of the violence to Wesley stopped, but his first visit to preach in Truro in 1762, a year after Walker's death, could have brought trouble. At least one man, a shoemaker called John Davey, went to West Bridge to hear him with stones in his pocket ready to use. But when the hymns were sung and prayers said he "began to feel that he was a good Man, and ere he began to Preach he began to empty his Pockets, quietly dropping them on the ground one by one."[41]

A small Methodist Society was started with a preaching house near the West Bridge. This was not large enough for the crowds that gathered to hear Wesley and there were several references in his diary to preaching in or just outside the Coinage Hall. In 1781, the time when he travelled to Truro through torrential rain, he wrote: "I have not for many years seen a congregation so universally affected. One would have imagined every one that was present had a desire to save his soul."

His last visit, in 1789, when he was eighty-six years old, was full of incident. He found Truro in tumult. Wesley wrote: "I could not get through the main street to our preaching house. It was quite blocked up with soldiers to the east, and numberless tinners to the west, a huge multitude of whom being nearly starved, were come to beg or demand an increase of their wages without which they could not live. So we were obliged to retire to the other end of the town, where I preached under the Coinage Hall to twice as many people, rich and poor, as the preaching house would have contained."[42]

One month earlier, on 14 July, the Bastille in Paris had been stormed, so beginning a revolution against the King's government. Many people in Britain welcomed it at first, regarding the French regime as too repressive and undemocratic, but unrest like this was frightening to the British Government which feared revolution spreading across the Channel. By 1793 Britain was at war with this dangerous country. The following years were full of incident for Truro people: war with France, unrest at home, hunger, death and victory. It was not until 1815 that Truro people were finally able to celebrate peace by turning out in force to give a hero's homecoming to the son of Betsy and John Vivian.

References

[1] Tregellas, 1894
[2] Griffiths, 1992
[3] Hawkridge, C., "Sarah of Trewarthenick", JRIC 1969
[4] Griffiths, op. cit.
[5] Jennings, Researches into the history of Truro (RIC)
[6] Palmer, 1990
[7] Tregellas, op. cit.
[8] ibid.
[9] Magnus Magnusson (ed.), *Biographical Dictionary,* Chambers, 1990
[10] *Royal Cornwall Gazette*, 30.8.06.
[11] McGrady, 1991
[12] ibid.
[13] Hawkridge, op. cit.
[14] Jennings, P., "The Expansion of Truro", JRIC XV
[15] Jennings, Researches
[16] Spreadbury, 1971
[17] Jennings, Researches
[18] Noall, 1963
[19] Jennings, Researches
[20] Jenkin, 1951
[21] Davidson, 1970
[22] Polwhele, 1836
[23] Tregellas, op. cit.
[24] Palmer, 1990
[25] Griffiths, op. cit.
[26] Hawkridge, op. cit.
[27] Jennings, Researches

[28] Davidson, op. cit.
[29] ibid.
[30] Tregellas, op. cit.
[31] Palmer (ed.), 1992
[32] *West Briton*, 28.3.1912
[33] Burton, E., *The Georgians at Home*, Longmans, 1967
[34] Jenkin, op. cit.
[35] Hitchens & Drew, *History of Cornwall*, 1824
[36] Hanson, J.& P., *To Clothe the Fields with Plenty*, Landfall Publications, 1997
[37] Spreadbury, op. cit.
[38] Polwhele, 1836
[39] Jenkin, op. cit.
[40] Douch, 1977
[41] Pearse, J., 1964
[42] ibid.

Chapter 7

Alarms, Hunger, Victory and Reform

A huge multitude of hungry miners on the march to Truro in the August of 1789 must have been a terrifying experience, when they poured down the steep hill, choking Kenwyn Street as they tried to ford the river and cross the bridge close to the town mill. No doubt shops were closed and boarded up in preparation, and the presence of armed soldiers would have been welcomed by Truro people. With this happening at their backs it was perhaps surprising that so many crowded round the Coinage Hall to listen to John Wesley, but perhaps he brought comfort to the frightened.

This was not the first time that Truro had been alarmed in this way. Two years earlier nearly a thousand had descended on the town "to pull their houses about their ears" as Admiral Boscawen's widow wrote, and there had been other times during the century when Truro or its neighbourhood seemed threatened, especially when a fall in the demand for tin or copper coincided with poor harvests and high prices for corn. In 1776 the *St James' Chronicle* described the miners as "very strange beings, half savages at best". It continued: "Many thousands of them live entirely underground, where they burrow and breed like Rabbits. They are rough as Bears, selfish as Swine, obstinate as Mules, and hard as the native Iron." Even if Truro people had less extreme and more accurate ideas about them, many might still have viewed them as a strange and different breed of men and therefore something to fear, especially in large numbers.

In 1787 the miners had been pacified by Lord Falmouth, the son of Admiral Boscawen, who was the owner of mines in Gwennap where many of these men worked. In 1789, with the dangerous events across the Channel worrying the authorities, the soldiers, who would have been far outnumbered by the miners, were ordered to fire on them but, as reported in the *Gentleman's Magazine*, "highly to their honour" they refused. James Watt, who had financial interests in the smooth working of the mines, reacted differently: "We had it in the newspapers that the military were desired to fire upon the Tinners but would not. I hope it is not so, otherwise we are going the same way as the French are, that is to the devil."[1] Seven years later soldiers did fire over the heads of the rioting tinners when they came to Truro and this time one of the leaders was hanged.

The miners could sometimes be persuaded to go home peaceably especially, as in 1766, when they were allowed to buy corn at pre-inflation prices. Richard Polwhele described the time in 1812 when a large group seized corn at Treliske just outside the town, and began threshing it and carrying it away with them. John Vivian of Pencalenick, as Sheriff, accompanied by Polwhele as a magistrate, appealed to their sense of right and wrong. Polwhele wrote: "Their leaders were ashamed of themselves; the flails and the sacks were abandoned and the crowds dispersed."[2] Scarcely the action of obstinate, selfish or hard men.

Truro also had its own poor who, since Tudor times, were a problem that the parish had to deal with. St Mary's parish had a small workhouse in St Clement Street which could not cope with the growing numbers, so in 1779 a new one was built near Henry Williams' almshouses (still a refuge in old age for a few) near the top of Pydar Street and close to the new prison recently built to replace the one opposite the Coinage Hall. One room in the poorhouse was to be used as a workshop for those who were experienced in spinning and weaving wool. Conditions could be drear, but they were kept fed and clothed after a fashion. Complaints were made about the quality of clothes supplied to them, and food was often based on potatoes or flour pudding, but meat was also given about three times a week. There were only ten people recorded there in 1803 but there were ten times that number receiving aid from the parish in their own homes.[3]

Individuals still gave help. Polwhele wrote of Parson Pye, the rector of St Mary's from 1761 to 1803: "Many were the halt, the blind - many were the poor destitutes whom he relieved by money and by clothes, as their necessities required, expending much more than the whole income of his living." He also commented on Dr John Wolcot, who "had always the milk of human kindness" and would "go dinnerless rather than send a poor man empty away". He added: "Alas! when he dispensed his medicines with such anxious attention to the sick - when he gave his bread to the hungry how much is it to be lamented that in his generous feelings ... there was no Christian principle!"[4]

Another doctor, William Pryce of Redruth, whose *Mineralogia Cornubiensis* was published in 1778, did not believe that the wealthy people of Cornwall were doing enough to help the poor. He recommended the building of a public hospital because of the frequent accidents suffered by miners. He wrote: "It is strange, that a county so large as Cornwall, so opulent, and abounding in so many accidents that require the greatest care and expertness in surgery, should be so long without a charity of this kind: I am sorry to observe, it is no proof of the wisdom and generosity of its nobility and gentry." He then added: "And as Redruth is situated on the narrowest part of the county, is the center *(sic)* of mining, and within two hours distance from our most frequented seaports; all these circumstances combine to prove the expediency of erecting a county hospital close by the town of Redruth." Twenty-one years later a Royal Infirmary for the poor was opened, with a male and a female ward totalling twenty beds, financed by public subscriptions, with George, the Prince Regent, heading the list of benefactors, and with Sir Francis Basset, Sir William Lemon and Sir John St Aubyn active in its promotion; but it was built in Truro not Redruth and so it was Truro people, not miners, who were most likely to benefit from this. (The name "Infirmary Hill" will presumably still remind people in the future of this impressive building which dominated the western side of the town, even after the City Hospital, as it later became, has closed and the site been redeveloped. See the engraving in Chapter 4, page 88.)

The wars against France intensified the problems, because Britain's rapidly growing population could no longer depend on imported wheat from Europe. Farmers reaped the benefits of the huge demand as prices soared. The poor suffered, and when harvests were particularly meagre because of wet weather, starvation was not far away. 1795 and 1796 were bad years. William Jenkin wrote: "We are in a distressed condition in this part of the country for want

The oldest part of the Royal Cornwall Infirmary

of Bread - such distress as I never saw before". A few months later in the winter of 1796 a committee was formed in Truro, including Ralph Allen Daniell, to encourage wealthier people to give money to buy barley to be ground at the town mill, which was then sold to the poor.

There were continuing fears that any disorders could increase the chance of revolution spreading to Britain. In March 1795 William Jenkin was writing about rioting amongst the miners of West Penwith: "I am told that in St Just they went so far, in imitation of our Gallic neighbours, as to plant the 'Tree of Liberty'." A friend of Richard Polwhele, who was then vicar of Manaccan, wrote to him that same month to calm his fears: "I think you may assure yourself than the sans-culottes will never lay a finger on the small or great tithes at Manaccan, or plant the tree of liberty in your churchyard, or the bonnet rouge on your head, or take away your breeches to cover their own credentials." Later in the year James Watt was advising William Murdoch, his engineer, to stay in Truro rather than Redruth for safety.

The difficulties suffered by the miners probably explain why so many signed up to serve in the Royal Navy under Captain Edward Pellew, when war broke out in 1793. Pellew was soon the talk of the town when his ship, the *Nymphe*, captured the first enemy frigate of the war in an action, described by the *Gentleman's Magazine* as "the most notable and awful that the naval history of the world ever recorded." This had been quite a Pellew family event, because on board with Edward was his younger brother, Israel, as well as his seven-year-old son, Pownall.

Nearly three years later Ned Pellew was again in the news for his heroic action at Plymouth. It was a wild night in January when a large merchant ship was driven on to rocks below the citadel. The only way to save the people trapped on board was to get a rope to them, but no-one was ready to risk the raging surf. Then Pellew arrived on the scene in full evening dress. His financial encouragement, to anyone brave enough to try, failed, so he seized the rope himself, swam out and saved over five hundred lives. Amongst the honours showered on him for this was a baronetcy. There was intense interest in the course of the war with the *Sherborne Mercury* printing the official news from commanders. In two consecutive weeks in August 1798 letters from Sir Edward Pellew were published on his capture of two French ships. One of these, *La Vaillante*, was advertised for sale a few months later in Plymouth, her abilities as a fast sailer proved by the number of prizes she had taken, and described as "the first vessel of the class to have been captured".

When plans were being made to set up Local Associations of men, the

Edward ("Ned") Pellew, Viscount Admiral Exmouth
From an engraving dated 1st September 1817
(Courtesy RIC)

"Dad's Army" of their day, to fight the French if they landed, some of the gentry were not sure of the wisdom of arming the working classes who might be encouraged to use the weapons against their masters, as the French were doing. There was also some uncertainty about who were the "enemy". The rector of Ruan Lanihorne suggested to his congregation that with these arms they would "be always prepared to give a warm reception to the tinners." Sir William Lemon was appointed Lieutenant-Colonel of the Royal Cornwall Militia, and Major Daniell commanded Truro's own Light Infantry Volunteers. In 1801 when the Truro Volunteers were reviewed by General Morshead he complimented this "fine body of young men" and said he would class them "among the most efficient and serviceable he had met in the course of his inspection."[5]

Every opportunity was taken to honour the victories, perhaps to take people's minds off the troubles at home. In October 1798 when Nelson defeated the French fleet anchored off the coast of Egypt, the *Sherborne Mercury* reported that there had been a celebration ball in Truro at the end of an exciting evening when "the Borough of Truro was most brilliantly illuminated, and various were the transparencies exhibited in honour of the late glorious victory obtained by Admiral Nelson over the French fleet. The evening was terminated by a very great display of fireworks and the utmost harmony and regularity was observed on the occasion." Transparencies, paintings probably on linen lit up from behind, were very popular at this time.

These celebrations would not have taken place if Cornelius Cardew, the schoolmaster and the chosen Mayor in 1797, had had his way, and some Truro people showed their feelings by breaking the windows of his house when he spoke out against them.[6] The welcome which many people had given the start of the revolution had quickly changed when events in France became nastily violent, so that Cardew was in a minority in opposing the war. In spite of his views his ten-year-old son, Octavius, had joined the navy as a midshipman in the *Amazon* under the command of another Truro man, Captain Robert Reynolds. In January 1797, he had experienced live action in a howling gale, being wrecked and then taken prisoner with his captain and the rest of the crew, but knowing that they had helped Edward Pellew destroy a French ship on the Breton coast in one of Pellew's most famous actions of the war.

The opening years of the new century again brought the threat of starvation with poor harvests and high prices. This time the Overseers of the Poor in Truro were given the powers to borrow from the banks to buy barley. William Jenkin wrote from his home in Redruth in January 1801: "The mine is dull and the Labourers are not able to do half the work they could a year ago. Near 100 of the men belonging to Tin Croft are now sick. I fear for want of nourishing food." Two months later he was writing: "Gwennap Mines pour forth their hundreds of desperate Labourers who can with great caution and difficulty be prevailed on to be quiet." This letter then had a hurried postscript. "Since I wrote this I have had the disgusting sight of a riotous assemblage of Tinners from Gwennap who broke into the market and are now compelling the people to sell Potatoes, Fish, Butter and Salt Pork etc. at the prices they choose to fix. Finding nobody to stop them (for we have neither Magistrate or Military here) they are likely to grow intoxicated both with Liquor and success - and I dread the consequence."

Truro had magistrates, and often soldiers billetted in the town, so was in a better position to defend itself. As early as 1773 the Town Council had asked Lord Falmouth to use his influence to try and have at least forty soldiers stationed permanently in the town.[8] Although this did not happen then, when soldiers were moved in from time to time they were billetted out in inns and private houses, and during the 1790s many local girls married soldiers, as many as twenty-three such weddings taking place in 1798 alone. Any more permanent arrangement seemed unnecessary when peace was declared in October 1801. Truro celebrated with a procession through the town by the workers at the carpet factory, the Truro Vounteers paraded and let off "three excellent vollies", transparencies were again on display and the evening was rounded off by a firework display, which was "truly superb".[9]

The peace was short-lived and when war broke out again in 1803 plans were made for building a temporary barracks in the fields at the top of Lemon Street. ("Barrack Lane" is now the only reminder of this.) The building was described in the proposed plan as an "additional ornament to this elegant little town from which will be enjoyed, in return, a most delightful prospect". The view, no doubt, was pleasant but Cornish rain found its way through the wood and plaster, and what was possibly worse, huge fleas soon infested the men's quarters, which had such vicious bites that soldiers found that sleeping with their horses in the stables was far more comfortable.[10] It was also noticeable that with the soldiers living in barracks the number of weddings to local girls dropped significantly.

Truro people were amongst the first in the country to hear about "a battle more tremendous and a conquest more glorious, than even the proud annals of the British navy could boast till now." This was the way that Truro's first newspaper, the *Royal Cornwall Gazette*, scooped its first and biggest story, Nelson's victory at Trafalgar in October 1805. The *Cornwall Gazette* and *Falmouth Packet* had been started in Falmouth in 1801 by Thomas Flindell, who has been described as "a man of quite extraordinary character, talents and originality". He moved to Truro in 1803 at the time when the war had started up again and when fears of an invasion of the country were at their most intense.

In 1805 Napoleon's plans for invasion had been fading, but he still hoped that the combined French and Spanish fleets could evade the British blockade of Cadiz. On 19 October, the British schooner *Pickle*, under the command of Lieutenant Lapenotiere, reported to Nelson that the enemy fleet was coming out of port. It was not until Monday 4 November that the *Pickle* sailed into Falmouth bringing the news of victory off Cape Trafalgar. The Lieutenant rode quickly through Truro on his way to London, not arriving there until the early hours of Wednesday morning. The *Royal Cornwall Gazette* reported: "When the news of this glorious victory first reached Truro, it was not saddened by that of Lord Nelson's death; it was therefore announced to the inhabitants by an illumination of the Subscription News-Room". But the report on 9 November, giving many details of the battle, included the news that "Lord Nelson is no more".

Two local men who survived the battle were Israel Pellew, Edward Pellew's younger brother who now commanded the *Conqueror*, and Richard Polwhele's son, Edward. In the early stages of the battle, when the French flagship was fighting Nelson's *Victory*, Captain Israel Pellew came to the support of his commander and shot away the enemy's sails leaving the Frenchman helpless, at which point he sent his Captain of Marine over to the stricken vessel to accept the surrender of the French admiral. This triumph for Pellew was never given full recognition; he was "the unsung hero of Trafalgar", as Michael Waters has written.[11]

Edward Polwhele was not in such an exalted position, but he had taken over command of his ship in the heat of the battle, when his Lieutenant had tried to board a prize. He wrote to his father: "I and the boatswain fired till our pieces became so hot we were obliged to drop them." He described the bravery of one of the crew who had been wounded and was being carried below to the surgeon "with all his bowels hanging out, encouraging his gunmates and huzzaing along the decks as he passed below." He concluded: "When I came out of action I could neither speak, nor hear, nor scarcely move."[12]

It was to be another ten long years before the fighting was finally over. Ten years in which bravery and sadness, hunger and victories were all to be experienced. The bravery of Richard Hussey Vivian, the son of Betsy and John Vivian, whose rearguard action in the retreat to Corunna in 1809 saved many British lives, earned him the thanks of Sir John Moore, the commander, who was killed soon afterwards. He himself narrowly escaped death on his return home, when the troopship he should have been on was wrecked in a storm on rocks near Coverack with the loss of nearly all the men. He and another Truro man had luckily accepted the invitation of a friend to travel on another ship, and so he lived to play his part in the victory of Waterloo.

Great sadness was felt at the death of Robert Reynolds, now an admiral, when his ship, the *St George*, sank in a horrific storm in the Baltic on Christmas Day 1811. Over five hundred men were lost including the Admiral's Clerk, William Hawken, the son of a Truro grocer, Midshipman Marshall, the son of a Truro surgeon, and Midshipman James, the son of a Truro lawyer. Truro was described as "almost like the land of Egypt when in every house there were wailings for the loss of the first born."[13]

How many Truro people forgot their troubles for a time to marvel at the exotic animals from the Royal Menagerie that arrived in the town two months later? "A stupendous male elephant", "a noble lion with a full mane", "the finest, most perfect and beautiful zebra that has been seen in this kingdom in the memory of man", "a noble panther", tigers, laughing hyenas and kangaroos, were some of the creatures advertised to be seen at High Cross for a fee. Ladies and gentlemen had to pay 2s, while "tradespeople etc" could view them for half that price.

That year there was once again the threat of real hunger after yet more bad harvests. In the Midlands and the North it resulted in the Luddite riots, when workmen destroyed the new machines which they believed were the cause of their unemployment and hunger. In Cornwall it was the miners who took action. The *Royal Cornwall Gazette* reported on 1 April 1812 that they "assembled in groups of considerable numbers in the quarter between Redruth and Truro, and then dispersed over the county with their empty sacks, to purchase corn from the farmers." Soon afterwards they began to trickle into Truro but "not riotously." Most of them were young men and boys or bal girls, who seemed to have come either for "curiosity or idleness", but although there was no rioting in the town the problem was severe, not only for the miners, and magistrates and others took action to deal with this.

In Truro the Overseers of the Poor in St Mary's parish bought up 280 sacks of Liverpool flour and recommended several poor families to join together to buy a sack to divide amongst themselves. People of the "upper and middling classes" were urged to reduce their consumption of flour which was regarded as "a solemn duty" which "no sound mind will evade". The *Gazette* published a recipe for rice crumpets to "husband our flour", and the Associated Attornies of the County of Cornwall, which assembled in Truro for the Easter Sessions, resolved to give up puddings or pastries at home to reduce their consumption of flour.

This was the year when the Prime Minister, Spencer Perceval, was assassinated, when Napoleon was forced to retreat from Moscow and when the Duke of Wellington was winning victories in Spain, the greatest being at Salamanca in July. Here was made the prized capture of several French standards, the Eagles, and Wellington sent Lord Clinton back to Britain to present them to the Government. He landed at Falmouth in August and then set off by carriage on the long road to London, stopping at Truro to change horses at Pearce's Hotel, the new name for the King's Head. The captured flags hung out of the windows of the carriage as crowds gathered around to admire them. One Truro merchant found the temptation too great; when he thought no-one was looking he cut off two of the golden tassels as a memento. There was immediately a commotion as someone accused him of the theft, which at first he strongly denied, but as the crowd became increasingly angry he sheepishly gave them back. No action was taken by Lord Clinton, whose first priority was to get them to London, but it was not forgotten by Truro people and ever after he had to suffer the nicknames of "Tommy Tassell" and "Salamanca Thomas."[14]

Another of Wellington's officers, Major George Henderson of the Royal Engineers, was sent to England with dispatches some time later, landing at Falmouth to start the long journey to London. For some reason he particularly remembered riding up the steep hill from Calenick, as he recalled to his children on many future occasions, little knowing that his son, James, would become familiar with this area when he came to settle in Truro in 1855 as a civil and mining engineer.[15]

Anyone visiting Truro at the end of July 1815 could well believe that the battle of Waterloo the previous month, which finally ended the long wars with France, had been won by General Sir Richard Hussey Vivian. He had played a vital part leading first the 10th and then the 18th Hussars, galloping into battle when Napoleon's veteran troops, the Imperial Guard who had been kept in reserve, at last advanced into the carnage of the battlefield. As the setting sun pierced through the smoke of the artillery Vivian's men charged into the French cavalry protecting the Old Guard and sent them scattering.

"Wellington, encouraged by the rapid and beautiful style in which Vivian's brigade advanced, and by the brilliant success of the attack, now ordered, amid the enthusiastic cheering of the troops, the long-looked-for general advance of the whole line," which Walter Tregellas described as then becoming a "march of triumph."[16]

Truro turned out in force to welcome their hero. As his carriage neared the town people flocked to meet him and escort him into his native town, where he arrived to a tumultuous reception, the carriage horses dispensed with in favour of the strong arms of many men who dragged him in triumph through the streets to his parents' house near the bottom of Pydar Street, on the site of what is now Union Place and Truro Methodist Church. There he was greeted by a select few, including one young girl, the mother of Walter Tregellas, whom he lifted up and kissed, saying: "There! believe me, that's the first kiss I've had since the battle of Waterloo." No mention is made in the reports of this time of either his wife or his mother. Eleven years earlier he had eloped to Gretna Green with his first wife, Eliza Crespigny, a marriage soon regularised by licence in Truro. His mother Betsy, so much admired by Richard Polwhele and John Wolcot, died eight months after this triumphal entry.

The celebrations were not over because a few days later the Assembly Rooms, decorated with flags, flowers, foliage, triumphal arches and "an elegant transparency from the ingenious pencil of Mrs Hempel",[17] was the scene for a splendid dinner of venison, turtle, peaches, melons and other exotic foods, washed down by champagne, madeira and claret. Sir Hussey, the guest of honour, arrived to the strains of the band of the Royal Cornwall Militia playing *Hail! The Conquering Hero Comes*, and when the toast to him was proposed "a burst of applause followed, which must have been truly gratifying, not only to the General himself, but equally so to his highly-respected father".

Nor was this all. A piano appeared and a glee was sung, composed by Charles Hempel, the organist of St Mary's and a popular concert performer, written in the flowery style of the time, which included these words.

> *Again War's Trump sends forth her brazen blast,*
> *And Britain's sons in battled ranks unite;*
> *They meet the daring foe, whose last*
> *Fell hope is ventured on the desp'rate fight.*
> *But vain his hope, where Wellington commands,*
> *Where British heroes form the warlike bands;*
> *And vain his hope to break the Phalanx dread*
> *By Picton, Uxbridge or by Vivian led.*

General Sir Richard Hussey Vivian
(Courtesy RIC)

163

Alarms, Hunger, Victory and Reform

The war with France might now be over, but there was one more victory for Truro people to applaud. The Barbary pirates of North Africa, who two hundred years earlier had caused such distress to Cornish people, were still causing problems in the Mediterranean area, including the capture and enslavement of Christians. Britain's power and influence in the Mediterranean had grown during the war and in 1816, Edward Pellew, soon to become Viscount Exmouth, was sent out to besiege the heavily-defended port of Algiers. His attack, which is regarded as perhaps his most celebrated exploit, destroyed the defences after a nine-hour battle which left the town and fortifications in ruins.

There were two other actions of his that local people could thank him for. One was the *saving* from destruction of a fort, this time nearer home. The Government had plans to demolish Pendennis Castle to save money, but he persuaded them to change their mind. Falmouth and then Truro also gained through him the services of a talented musician, the negro Joseph Emidy, but whether he would have thanked Pellew is another matter.

The extraordinary story of this man has been told by Richard McGrady in *Music and Musicians in early Nineteenth Century Cornwall.* By his early twenties he had been taken from his home on the Guinea coast of West Africa, was sold into slavery in Brazil and was then brought to Lisbon where his master encouraged his musical talents to such an extent that he played the violin in the orchestra at the opera house. It was here in the Portuguese capital that Captain Pellew saw him in 1795, when his damaged ship was being refitted, and Pellew gave orders for the kidnapping of this young man so that his sailors could be entertained by light music and dances. For nearly four years he was kept as a prisoner on board. He must have learnt to recognise the cliffs and coves of Cornwall as Pellew sailed in and out of his base at Falmouth for his patrols of the Channel, and it was in Falmouth that he was finally granted his freedom in 1799.

There James Silk Buckingham, who was later to be active in the campaign against the slave trade, met him as a music teacher. He described him as being "an exquisite violinist, a good composer, who led at all the concerts of the county, and who taught equally well the piano, violin, violoncello, clarionet and flute."[18] Joseph must have been accepted by the local people because he married Jenefer Hutchins, the daughter of a respectable tradesman, and they had several children, at least two of whom showed musical ability: Thomas who became a cabinet maker and the leader of a Quadrille Band, and Cecilia, their only daughter, who in 1822 made her debut when she was thirteen years old as a singer in the Assembly Rooms in Truro. "*Robin Adair* was prettily

"A Musical Club", Truro, 8th November 1808.
The violinist is Joseph Emidy.   (Courtesy RIC)

sung by a new debutant, Miss Emidy, and encored by the audience," the *Royal Cornwall Gazette* recorded. The family had moved to Truro some years earlier and here Joseph lived until his death in 1835. He featured prominently in the musical life of the town playing at the Town Hall, the Assembly Rooms, and in private houses with the gifted amateurs of the Harmonic Society, composing and teaching. The verse on his tombstone in Kenwyn Churchyard reads:

> *Devoted to thy soul inspiring strain*
> *Sweet Music! thee he haild his chief delight*
> *And with fond zeal that shunn'd not toil nor pain*
> *His talent soar'd and genius marked his flight.*

War can bring radical changes to both individuals and nations. Joseph Emidy would probably never have come to Cornwall if it had not been for the war, and the privations of the war with fears of revolution helped to bring about much-needed reforms in Britain. One reform during the war must have had Emidy's approval. In 1807 slave trading was made illegal in Britain, but in spite of this many British ships still continued with this lucrative commerce. It was not until twenty-five years later, two years before Emidy died, that an

Act was finally passed to abolish slavery in all British-controlled lands. This had been a long fight against vested interests, but other political battles were also being fought during these years, of more direct concern to many Truro people.

Fellow Townsmen!

In the annals of your Borough, the present is, perhaps, the most eventful period. You will soon have an opportunity afforded you of exercising the most valuable privilege which can appertain to Englishmen, and which has been, so unjustly, withheld from you, namely - that of sending Members, of your own choice, to represent you in the first Reformed Parliament of the British Empire.

This letter, written to the *Royal Cornwall Gazette* by an "inhabitant-householder of Truro" on 1 June 1832, signalled the imminent passing of a Parliamentary Act which, at long last, would give the vote to many more men. In Truro, until this time, only twenty-five men had this right, the Mayor, Aldermen and Capital Burgesses, and in the last contested election only eleven of them had voted.

Not surprisingly, most of this Corporation, as well as others under Boscawen influence, opposed the suggested change. (The Councillors were soon to find their powers further eroded when, in 1835, a reform of Town Councils to make them more accountable to the ratepayers, resulted in few of them being elected to serve on the new Borough Council.) The ground swell of support for the Reform Act was strong in Truro, as in many other parts of the country. In early May, when hopes had been dashed and then joyfully raised over the Government's ability to pass the Act, Truro people flocked into the streets and danced as a band paraded through the town in triumph before an impromptu meeting was held on the Green, with speakers standing on rickety tables, stirring up the hopes of hundreds of people crowding around.

Truro's two newspapers added to the furore by each supporting a different side, the newer one, the *West Briton*, advocating reform while the *Gazette* upheld the traditional view. At one stage the Reformers were so angry with the *Gazette* that they made a bonfire on Castle Hill with copies of the offending issues and kept the town in uproar throughout the evening. (The *West Briton* had been started in 1810 under the editorship of Edward Budd, who moved from Liskeard to start this new enterprise in Truro, the social centre of the county. It was printed and published by John Heard, but by the time of the furore over the Reform Act, it was his widow, Elizabeth, who had been doing this for nine years and she became known as "Cornwall's most able amiable business woman".)

On 7 June 1832 the crowds were out again early in the morning to meet the Royal Mail coach, as it galloped into the town to delighted cheers carrying the news that the Act had finally been passed. Cornwall lost many of its MPs, so reducing its influence in Parliament, but Truro still kept the right to have two Members. Nearly four hundred male householders in Truro now gained the franchise; not many, but it was a step in the right direction and one that had been bitterly fought for. This was not the end of the matter, because new elections now had to be held and the reformers were determined to be represented.

Celebrations for the passing of the Reform Act could well be regarded as part of the election campaign. Mr Tooke, the reform candidate, was soon making a triumphal entry into the town, accompanied by horsemen and music, riding through streets decorated with arches and houses festooned with flags and greenery. He spent four days in the town canvassing and then left "amidst the hearty cheers of a large concourse of Electors."

The ladies of Truro were invited to a public tea party by his supporters. Tables were laid along Pydar Street where they took their refreshments, watched by an enormous crowd, and entertained by music from a band perched on a triumphal arch, the day being rounded off with fireworks. In August the town was decorated once again, a band played, beef was distributed to the poor and any others recommended by the committee, and a splendid dinner was arranged in Philip Sambell's timber yard by Back Quay, with a huge bonfire and a firework display from a barge moored in the river. A potentially inflammatory occasion in more ways than one!

When the elections were finally held in November there was, as was usual then, no secret ballot and it took three days to gain the final result. The hustings were erected at High Cross where the three candidates stood, one reformer, Mr Tooke, one anti-reformer, Mr John Ennis Vivian, and one who was neutral, Sir Richard Hussey Vivian, the hero of Waterloo, who had already represented Truro for a time after the wars. On the first day the Mayor, who was in charge of the proceedings, took a show of hands from the electors crowding around the platform. His declaration was challenged by Ennis Vivian's supporters and a poll was demanded, which the Mayor stated would start the following morning. Three polling booths were erected and by the end of the second day seventy-six men had withheld their vote, so that evening there was plenty of behind-the-scenes activity as "persuasion" of all kinds was being used by the supporters of both sides. By the end of the third day, excitement was intense. A crowd of several thousand had gathered in the fading light to watch the Mayor ceremoniously hold up the books recording the votes and then break the seals. There was complete silence as he announced the results, then cheers and shouts echoed in the dusk when Sir Hussey's name topped the poll by a large majority, followed by Mr Tooke, who was then carried aloft through the streets to an enthusiastic response. Sir Hussey declined a similar progress but instead gave £100 to be distributed in coal and provisions for the poor, a gesture no doubt appreciated by those people who still had no right to vote. As his memorial tablet in the Cathedral states: "His charity, benevolence and integrity endeared him to all who knew him: the widow and orphan never appealed to him in vain and the deserving soldier always found him a friend."

He has no other memorial in Truro, but another Truro man, Richard Lemon Lander, who died in 1834 far away from Truro, has a fine memorial overlooking his native town. "The Truro folk mean to erect a pyramid, or a cenotaph, or a school-room, or a conventicle - the Lord knows what or where - in commemoration of Lander and his brother," wrote Polwhele.[19] Richard was born in February 1804, on the day when Colonel John Lemon, Sir William's brother, was elected MP for Truro, hence his middle name. Polwhele recalled his birthplace at the entrance to the Green which at the time of writing in the 1830s was an inn called the Dolphin, but then "had the sign of the Fighting Cocks, an inn kept by their father, still living - a much esteemed servant of the Daniells". The constant bustle on the quays, the thirsty sailors calling impatiently for their drinks in the bar with its dark, oak benches, the farmers stabling their market carts in the large inn courtyard, the miners crowding in at

The Dolphin Buttery, now demolished, occupied the building which was once the Fighting Cocks Inn. The carving of the dolphin is now in Boscawen Park. (Photograph courtesy John James)

coinage times, all provided the backdrop to the lives of the young Lander children. Although Richard earned a reward from his schoolteacher for his work, he was just as liable to wander off to listen the sailors' stories of exciting foreign lands.[20]

    About the time that his father became bankrupt, in 1813, young Richard set out to walk to London and begin his own adventures. He went with a merchant to the West Indies, became a servant to wealthy London families who sometimes travelled on the continent, and then he had the opportunity of going to Africa. It was his experience of West Africa that took him back there again, with the support of the Government, to unravel the "mystery of the Niger", to explore the lower reaches of the Niger and discover where this great river entered the sea. This time he was accompanied by his younger brother, John, a compositor in the offices of the *Royal Cornwall Gazette*. They succeeded in proving that rivers on the coast of the Bight of Benin were part of the huge delta complex of the Niger.[21] They returned safely after many adventures, difficulties and dangers, but Richard died on his third voyage of discovery after being wounded in a fight. It was then that Truro people decided on the memorial (shown right in a photograph by John James).

    In June 1835 a solemn

procession walked up Lemon Street, a small girl, Richard's daughter, being led by the hand, for the laying of the foundation stone of a tall pillar to be built at the top of the hill (where the hated barracks had recently been demolished). Almost a year afterwards, when the pillar was near completion, it collapsed, possibly because of an earth tremor. Polwhele wrote: "I heard it fall to the ground with a portentous crash that shook all Lemon Street." Before it was rebuilt John had also died from an illness contracted on his one expedition, so his name was also included on the memorial. Eventually, in 1852, a statue of Richard was placed on the top of the column, carved by Nevil Northey Burnard, Cornwall's skilled sculptor. Although Burnard had never seen Lander he was anxious that the statue should look like him, so he first made use of a portrait owned by the Royal Geographical Society and then realised that Lander's daughter had very similar features so he also used her face as a model.

Richard's determination, bravery and success had already been recognised by the Royal Geographical Society, which had awarded him its first gold medal in 1832. In the Society's chapel of the Savoy in London a tablet was erected to his memory, which was destroyed by fire in 1864. A stained glass window was then installed, only for that to be destroyed by bombs during the Second World War.[22] Now there seems to be no reminder in London of this intrepid explorer. One hundred years after his death, in 1934, Truro people remembered him by a ceremony around the garlanded column (see the photograph opposite) and by the production of commemorative mugs painted with his likeness.

Another man hitting the headlines during the 1830s was John Nichols Tom, who had been born in St Columb, educated in Penryn and became a clerk to a Truro wine and spirits merchant in the 1820s before taking over the business himself as a maltster and hop dealer, with premises in Pydar Street. In 1828 these burned down, and with his suspiciously high insurance pay-out he rebuilt them "in a commodious manner." Not long afterwards he travelled to Liverpool with a cargo of malt, which he sold for £1,000, and with that he set off on his adventures, his behaviour becoming more and more erratic. (His mother, "cracked" Charity, had died in the County Lunatic Asylum[23] and he obviously inherited some of her mental instability.) He travelled widely in Europe, Turkey and Palestine, and when he returned to England as a "Knight of Malta" he called himself, amongst other names, Sir William Courtenay. He stood for Parliament in Canterbury being defeated by a few votes, but then he was indicted for perjury in a smuggling trial and only escaped transportation by the intervention of his wife and other Truro friends, who put him into the Kent

Asylum. After his release he declared himself "the Messiah", stirred up a riot against the new Poor Laws, which were very unpopular, and in a skirmish in June 1838 shot a constable and a soldier and was then shot himself. That month the *Gazette* reported on the auction sale of his "handsome and respectable" furniture from his house in Pydar Street.

The new Poor Laws, which were so disliked, also had their effect in Truro, where the old poorhouses and workhouses were replaced with a new, larger building at the top of Tregolls Road to serve the new Truro Poor Law Union. Here in the Bastille, as many of these institutions were called, the poor were "looked after", where children could be separated from their parents and husbands from their wives, where work might be provided that could be hard and painful, where there was a sufficiency of food for a life which some felt was not worth living. To be poor seemed almost a crime, a fault of their own making.

Another change that happened was one peculiar to Truro and the other coinage towns. The system of coinage, that had controlled so much of the tin trade since the Middle Ages, was finally abolished in October 1838, partly thanks to Lewis Charles Daubuz, chairman of a combination of the Cornish smelters. He was probably the most important tin smelter at the time, who had acquired two smelting houses in Truro: Carvedras once owned by the Rosewarnes, and the Truro Smelting Works, which had started in 1816 close to the confluence of the River Allen with the Truro river. He also had interests

A sketch from A Remembrance of Truro *in the Bishop's Library. Entitled "Fore Street, Truro", it shows the bank that replaced the Coinage Hall.*

in others at St Austell and St Erth, so he was an influential voice in the argument against the restrictive coinage system. The expenses involved had greatly increased since the early eighteenth century accounts for the Newham smelting works. At the Xmas Coinage of 1829 porterage had increased to £4 10s 6d, the payment for the work of both the poiser and numerator was now 16s 6d, as was "In and Out of Scales", and "Hammer" cost 10s 6d. There were a number of other costs, for individuals, for candles, stationery, postage, coals and carriage, and a "Gift" of £4.[24] The growing dissatisfaction with the system finally brought its demise.

The old Coinage Hall, now redundant, stood in the centre of the town for another ten years, but was then knocked down for the erection of a bank in the building that can still be seen at the eastern end of Boscawen Street. The Cornish Stannary Parliament had already had its last meeting there over eighty years earlier, in 1753, but the Vice-Warden's meetings continued, with sessions now held in the Town Hall; a building which was also soon to be replaced. Impressive structures, some already built and others to be erected, were changing the face of the town during these years of the nineteenth century which were to see the borough change its status. Truro was to become a city.

References

[1] Jenkin, 1927
[2] Polwhele, 1826
[3] Palmer (ed.), 1992
[4] Polwhele, 1836
[5] *Royal Cornwall Gazette*, 1801
[6] Palmer, 1990
[7] Jenkin, 1951
[8] Palmer, 1990
[9] *Royal Cornwall Gazette*
[10] Douch, 1977
[11] Palmer (ed.), 1992
[12] Polwhele, 1826
[13] Palmer (ed.), 1992
[14] Jennings, Researches
[15] *Traverser*, the magazine of the Henderson mining school (RIC)

[16] Tregellas, 1894
[17] *Royal Cornwall Gazette*
[18] McGrady, 1991
[19] Polwhele, 1836
[20] Tregellas, 1894
[21] Mackay, M., *The Indomitable Servant*, Rex Collings, 1978
[22] ibid.
[23] Douch, 1977
[24] Jennings, Researches

Chapter 8

Festivals, Fevers, Fires and Floods

Triumphal arches, a service, processions, bands, the firing of cannon, hundreds of children marshalled into order for a march down Lemon Street to sing to crowds of excited people outside the church at High Cross, fireworks and dancing into the night, all marked Truro's celebrations for the coronation of the young Queen Victoria on 28 June 1838, the year after she succeeded to the throne. This was a month for enjoyment because only three weeks earlier the Whitsun Fair had been held in warm, sunny weather, when the cattle trade had been brisk, the theatrical entertainments varied, two magnificent elephants, a "den of lions" and other exotic creatures had drawn huge crowds, and the inns had done a roaring trade. This weather was in marked contrast to three months earlier when piercing winds and snow had swept the county, making the Exeter mail coach two days late, nearly killing the driver of the Penzance mail-cart who had to be dug out of his snow-embedded vehicle and forcing all Truro shops to close early leaving the streets deserted.

After the Fair the *Royal Cornwall Gazette* reported that "the pick-pockets were on the alert but so were the constables and we do not hear that any robberies were committed." A series of burglaries in the town was causing concern at this time. In April, after yet another break-in had been reported in the *Gazette*, the paper added: "The constables are using their best endeavours to trace the offenders: but it is really high time that the inhabitants should stir themselves. The town is growing very rapidly in size; and some care should be taken to prevent its growing still more rapidly in vice and crime." Six months later the Town Council resolved: "That it is necessary to render the constabulary force more efficient." A Police Inspector was appointed "free from all local connections" and two constables were to be selected to act as a night watch with another by day as a street keeper.

Despite this modernisation of the police system, the *West Briton* reported disapprovingly in October 1844 on the use of a medieval form of punishment. "Two women, old and notorious drunkards, were placed in the stocks under sentence for 6 hours, we believe, in the middle of Boscawen Street, opposite the market gates. One employed herself with knitting, apparently indifferent to the hundreds of people and children standing around her. The other woman

175

was distressed and wept continually. For the last 50 years such an occurrence has not been known in Truro and we hope it will not occur again."

The population was growing steadily. In 1801, when the first census was taken, the parish of St Mary's, Truro, had 2358 people, and when the area of the town in Kenwyn and St Clements was added the total came to 4338. In 1824 F.W.L. Stockdale wrote: "The parish of St Mary's Truro contains, according to the late returns, 2712 inhabitants, an increase of 230 since the year 1811; but if the adjoining parishes of St Clement's and Kenwyn were included, the amount would be considerably augmented."[1] In the early 1830s the Parliamentary borough had over eight thousand people, with most of these in the town. This increase led to overcrowding and the need to build more houses. There was infilling in the town with dark courts built behind the main streets, but houses also began to be built along the steep valley sides to the north with terraces such as Rosewin Row, Paul's Row and St Clement's Terrace.

Two of the lion-head carvings in Walsingham Place, which was built as part of the infilling during these years.

Two reports in the newspapers of 1838 indicate yet other changes in progress. In February a jury assembled at Pearce's Hotel to assess the compensation to be paid to Miss Ferris for a part of a tenement owned by her which was needed to make the "proposed New Street at the Western end of the town." In June the Town Council resolved "to allow the river near the West Bridge to be diverted, for the better laying out of the new street leading into Ferris Town." John Ferris, who carried on the family tanning business in Pydar Street, and his cousin Josephus, a banker, were largely responsible for the development of the western part of the town below the old castle. At first the access to these

Window details of a house in River Street

new houses was from narrow Kenwyn Street, but more ambitious plans were put into operation by diverting the course of the River Kenwyn, putting part of it underground and building the much wider road of River Street leading to the West Bridge.

Philip Sambell, the son of the timber merchant with premises by the Kenwyn river, was the architect for some of the most impressive buildings erected during these years. He must have been a man of extraordinary talent and determination, because he was both deaf and dumb, and yet he drew up plans for the Ferris's development, planned both the Baptist Church in River Street and the Savings Bank next door (now the home of the Royal Institution and the Royal Cornwall Museum), designed, in 1830, St Mary Clement Church, "the Methodist Cathedral" in what had been the gardens of John Vivian's house, planned the elegant row of houses along Strangways Terrace on the site of the barracks, designed the Lander memorial column, as well as two churches, St John's at the top of Lemon Street, and St Paul's in Agar Road, which was rebuilt later in the century. "He has left a legacy in Truro for us all to admire."[2]

St Mary Clement, now Truro Methodist Church

The building of these two churches, and later St George's, is another indication of the demands of the growing population. The land for St John's church was given by Sir Charles Lemon, son of Sir William who had died in 1824, and the foundation stone was laid on 5 April 1827 by Thomas Daniell, the son of Ralph Allen Daniell, who was soon to be declared bankrupt. When the church opened the following year it had room to accommodate 800 poor people in the free pews in the nave. It is likely that the solicitors and doctors who were soon to live nearby in Strangways Terrace would have their carriages to take them to Kenwyn church, but the families of the washerwomen, tin

Strangways Terrace in the early 1960s (Courtesy John James)

smelters, the groom, the sadler and the butcher, who were recorded in the 1841 census living just below in Lemon Row, would now have a convenient place of worship, if they were Anglicans.

The power and influence of the Anglican church were being increasingly questioned, in particular the money that had to be paid to it by people who already supported their own churches financially. This produced a riot in Truro in 1838. When the goods of three men were due to be auctioned to pay for their church rates a crowd began to gather outside the auctioneer's premises. As the sale started there was first of all hooting and booing and then some of the crowd surged forward, knocked the auctioneer off his stool, and tore the clothes off his back. The sale was stopped, but when the auctioneer was prepared to try again in the afternoon a larger crowd assembled at the call of a bugle, broke down his door and rushed in. The auctioneer managed to slip out, minus his hat and coat, to get help from the Mayor, who in fact did very little. That evening the crowds were out on the streets with stones to break the auctioneer's windows. Five men were arrested and were given one month's imprisonment, three of them also paying a fine of £25 each. When they returned to Truro after their release they entered the town in triumph in a chaise and four with a band playing, surrounded by a "body of Chartists and a mob of boys and other idle people", as reported by the disapproving *Royal Cornwall Gazette*.

Festivals, Fevers, Fires and Floods

The mention of "Chartists" is a reference to the movement amongst some of the working classes to gain the vote and make politicians more accountable to the people. A Charter of six points was drawn up in London that year, mainly the responsibility of the Cornishman William Lovett, who had left the county some years earlier for work in the capital. Over the next ten years these Chartists were to cause the Government some trouble, especially in the worst times of hunger and unemployment.

There were other problems at this time, such as the overcrowding in the Market House, which was soon to be rectified. John Tonkin, who lived in Lemon Row with his wife, Mary, and their four children, was one of fifty-five butchers in 1840, all but one of whom traded in the weekly market in Boscawen Street.[3] This seems an extraordinarily large number, as compared with the eighteen grocers and one fruit merchant recorded at that time. The market must have been a Mecca for the dogs of the town. In 1839 the *West Briton* reported on "the nuisance to which inhabitants of Boscawen Street are weekly subjected, by dogs being left in the market house, after the butchers and others leave it, the yells of these animals being most distressing, particularly to invalids, when heard in the still hour of night."

This was not the only cause for concern because of dogs. Richard Polwhele, writing at the beginning of the century, referred to the large number of instances of rabies in the west of England and mentioned a case in Truro when a young child had been bitten by a mad dog and was "smothered between two feather-beds, in the last extremities of this dreadful disease."[4] When summer approached the danger of rabies increased and orders were often issued for all dogs to be muzzled. In June 1832 the *Gazette* was urging: "As the season is at hand when dogs may be expected to exhibit those symptoms of hydrophobia, to which every year some persons fall victim...it would be well if persons who keep dogs would either chain them to their kennels, or at least provide them with muzzles and plenty of water." The first action of the newly-reformed Town Council in 1835 was to give notice that all stray dogs would be destroyed, and a great number were seized as a result.

These were not the only nuisances on the streets. Clement Carlyon, a highly respected Truro doctor, wrote: "When the alarm of cholera prevailed great exertions were made to keep off so dreaded a calamity. Additional scavengers were appointed, not merely to sweep the streets more carefully, but to remove nuisances from outlets and close passages." These "nuisances" were caused by the lack of adequate sewerage, with open drains bringing "oozings of pig sties and other filth to stagnate at the foot of walls". Other sewers stopped short of the rivers with all the filth collecting in catchpits which "finally open on the surface, frequently in some street or lane, where a neglected deposit of a mixed animal and vegetable nature is allowed to become a possible source of annoyance or mischief." It seems a miracle that Truro did not suffer from the terrible first epidemic of cholera in 1832, which took its toll of many other towns in Cornwall. Although the cause of the disease was not definitely known, the Town Council responded to the threat, not only by better cleaning of the streets and diverting water from the leats through the gutters to carry away dirt, but also by building more sewers, and these actions possibly saved the town. The *Gazette* was able to report in November: "Truro has escaped from the visitation, not a single fatal case of cholera having occurred in the town. Is not this a cause for public thanksgiving?"

When Dr. Charles Barham wrote a report on the "Sanatory *(sic)* State of Truro" in 1840, partly based on Dr. Clement Carlyon's findings, he drew attention to Carlyon's comments on the improvements made to the area west of Pydar Street, Coombes Lane and Tippet's Backlet, by giving them a supply of running water. They were once "scarcely ever free from fever" but were now "among the healthiest parts of the town". Barham praised the airy rows of well-built cottages on Paul's Row (pictured below) and St Clement's Terrace, but condemned the "ignorance, cupidity or negligence of landlords". He

Coombes Lane still has its supply of running water.

continued: "It is useless to have a good sewer carried through the centre of the street, if the houses at the sides, and still more those situated in courts and lanes adjoining, have no communicating drains", and he regretted that with "the removal of the panic" the efforts made against cholera in 1832 were not continued. Carlyon had condemned the upper part of Pydar Street and Goodwives' Lane as "wretchedly unwholesome", and the houses in the St Clement area of the town as "objectionable habitations", but he also had this to say about Truro's most elegant street. "Who would suppose that so fine a street as Lemon-street was destitute of a common sewer?" Although Barham indicated that some improvements had been made, he highlighted some of the problem areas, such as the "abominable filthy state of the back premises" of the houses on the south side of Charles Street, where removal of such "horrible nuisances" would be difficult to cope with because of "the nature of the ground and wretched construction of the houses."

Dr Barham recorded the average age of death in Truro as thirty-one years, but with a marked difference between the classes. For professional people and gentry the average age was forty-four, for tradesmen thirty-six and for the labourers, who had the worst living conditions, twenty-nine. When reports of a low typhus fever had appeared in the papers in 1838 it was "chiefly confined to the crowded dwellings at the foot of Mitchell Hill and in the neighbouring streets." The *Gazette* added: "We do not learn that it has invaded any of the more open and airy parts of the town." Richard and John Lander's elder brother, James, died from a typhus epidemic at this time.

In 1847 Lord Falmouth praised the improvements that were being made and gave Dr. Clement Carlyon, who was Mayor for three years running, due recognition for them: "When I look round and see the admirable state in which your streets are ... I know it is mainly to him you owe these sanitary regulations which I trust will prove so beneficial to your town."[5] Perhaps he was being too complacent because when cholera struck again two years later Truro did not completely escape the scourge, and Mitchell Hill was one of the areas affected, although the epidemic was less fatal here than in towns like Hayle and Mevagissey. Nationally over 2,279 people were recorded as dying from cholera in one week in August when in Truro there were five, but others who had contracted the disease were reported to be recovering.

Improvements to sewerage and water supplies were constantly being urged, especially by doctors like Carlyon and Barham, but the Councils were reluctant to spend the money. In 1852 Dr. Barham was strongly supporting the building of reservoirs at Daubuz Moors to provide the town with a better water supply, with wash houses and bath houses for the poor, but nothing was done. Horrific findings of sewage contamination in the wells over the following years, with a Government Inspector's report in 1872 showing that water from twelve wells carried ten times more more solid matter in them than London's main sewer, the River Thames, eventually brought some action.[6] People might well have been safer drinking the soda water, which started to be made in Truro in 1839, where a steam engine was used to purify the "delicious and refreshing drink...(which) can be equalled but by few and excelled by none in the world."[7]

When Lord Falmouth praised Dr. Clement Carlyon in 1847, he added: "I find that Dr. Carlyon has been mixed up with every useful and praiseworthy institution connected either with this town, or its immediate neighbourhood." This was said on a day of great festivity when two of these "praiseworthy institutions" had their grand opening: the new Town Hall and Market House.

Truro Town Hall & Markets: a nineteenth-century engraving
(Courtesy RIC)

On 5 November 1847 a band headed a long procession of people led by Dr. Carlyon, Lord Falmouth and Mr Gregor of Trewarthenick, who had taken the maiden name of his wife, Sarah, when she became the sole heiress. They left the Red Lion to walk to St Mary's church for a service in the morning. Then in the afternoon they all gathered again, this time at the Assembly Rooms, to process to the impressive new Town Hall and Market in Boscawen Street, built partly on the site of the earlier one which had lasted for less than forty years. They solemnly entered the building and climbed the grand staircase, "the excitement occasioned by this formal opening...being heightened by the unexpected effect of the music, with its reverberating echoes, rolling in full and almost overpowering harmonies around the spacious building, its lofty ceilings and beautiful corridor."[8] In all this ceremony the ladies took no part except as spectators. Even when the dignitaries all trooped downstairs to the Market Hall where rows of tables were laid out for a dinner, the ladies were not included, but after the dinner they were allowed in to be "interested spectators and attentive listeners" to the speeches.

Twenty five years after the opening Polsue described the new building as having "an elegant modern Italian front, surmounted with a turret containing an illuminated clock with four dials, the present of L.J.Dampier,Esq., late Vice-Warden of the Stannaries. Besides the general market-place on the ground floor, the structure comprises the Town Hall, Council Chamber, the Offices of the Stannaries, the Police Station, the offices of the Fire Brigade etc." He also stated that "the "extensive and well-arranged Market House" had been erected at considerable cost. In his speech on the day of the opening Dr. Carlyon had begun: "I feel it to be my duty to vindicate an expenditure which would only be justified by the urgent requisitions of a rapidly increasing community." He later added: "Fortune favors *(sic)* the bold", which could be the motto today, because in the mid-1990s this striking granite building, in urgent need of vital structural repairs, has undergone huge changes to its interior to make it into "The Hall for Cornwall". The official opening in November 1997 is one hundred and fifty years after the original opening ceremony, when Dr Carlyon also referred to other ambitious plans for the town.

The entry into Truro from the east by New Bridge Street had been causing problems for many years because of the sharp bends that coaches had to make. Four people had been killed and many other accidents recorded, so plans were made to make a new bridge over the River Allen to bring traffic into the town by Prince's Street. One of the first meetings in the new Town Hall, in January 1848, was to hold an enquiry into the problems that could be caused to river traffic if this bridge were to be built. There were several merchants who operated above the site of the proposed bridge from quays on the River Allen, which was still navigable for vessels up to 50 tons.

The Round House at the corner of New Bridge Street and St Austell Street: its shape was an attempt to help coaches turn the sharp bend.

Joseph Carne was one of the largest operators from this area, with an extensive flour and grocery business at East Bridge. He said that the landing place there was good but at that time trade was poor so he was not using it. (1848 was one of the bad years of the decade which have become known as "the hungry forties".) The other important merchant here was Robert Michell, who dealt in lime, coal, timber and lead from his premises in Old Bridge Street. He was one of the most important merchants at that time with a fleet of vessels as well as interests in East Wheal Rose near St Newlyn East, the lead ore being carried from there to Truro down Mitchell Hill to his quay on the Allen. He also had a lead smelting works at Point, further south on the Fal estuary. A one-masted barge regularly carried the ore to his quay there, which was his main shipping place. He said that he could not risk using a vessel with a jointed mast (to get under the proposed bridge) carrying a cargo of lead across Falmouth Harbour in a gale.

In spite of these objections Boscawen Bridge was built, the Earl of Falmouth laying the foundation stone in November 1848 for a wooden structure on stone piers. The day was cold and wet and the Earl had to climb down a

*Truro from Poltisco: an engraving showing the first Boscawen Bridge.
See also pages 10 and 12. (Courtesy Cornish Studies Library)*

ladder to officially lay the first stone in the bed of the river. Nothing daunted
he did this, after a speech in which he commented favourably on all the building
being done in the town which showed "how very much the spirit of architecture
has improved."

The building of the bridge over the River Allen reduced boat access into
the town so that Truro, which had developed as a port in the Middle Ages, was
slowly loosening its ties with the sea. The silting up of the Truro river was also
creating real problems for shipping and several suggestions were put forward
over the years to improve the situation, but none of the radical ideas was adopted
because of the expense involved. In spite of the difficulties coastal trade was
brisk, especially the trade with South Wales on the copper and coal run. Truro
also had its own shipping company with regular runs to and from London, and
the Shipping Reports in the papers indicated the number of boats coming in
from other ports, such as Gloucester, Liverpool, Southampton and Sunderland.
A few crossed the Atlantic from Canada and others came from Norway bringing
timber, and timber yards and ponds extended along the waterfront of the Truro
River. The Reverend Francis Kilvert later commented on the Danish and
Norwegian ships anchored down-river from Truro near Malpas, when he visited

TRURO
SHIPPING COMPANY.

NOW LOADING,

At Symons's Wharf, Southwark, London,

THE GOOD SHIP

CAROLINE,

CAPTAIN HICKS,

DIRECT for TRURO,

And will sail within 14 days with Goods and Passengers, for Truro, Redruth, Camborne, Saint Agnes, Tregony, Helston, Breage, Gwennap, Chacewater, St. Day, Bodmin, Saint Austell, Saint Columb, Padstow, Wadebridge, Grampond, Falmouth, Penryn, Flushing, St. Mawes, and all Places adjacent.

☞ *Vessels will regularly succeed each other at the above Wharf.*

Truro, March 21, 1815.

the area in 1870. "They had brought timber and were waiting to take back miscellaneous cargoes, among other things, tin and copper."[9]

The rivers Kenwyn and Allen flowing through the centre of the town were losing their commercial uses as they were being bridged, confined and even covered over, but from time to time they could still make sure that they were not completely ignored, and December 1848, a month after the opening of Boscawen Bridge, was one of these occasions. The wet weather of November continued into December and the rivers became swollen. Soon after Christmas they were overflowing and the lower parts of the town were under a few inches of water. Truro had known floods before and was to experience many more afterwards but these proved to be some of the most destructive, because with little warning the waters suddenly rose four or five feet and in some parts near the West Bridge the depth was nearly six feet. Perhaps all the new building had made the situation worse. Two carriage houses at the back of Pearce's Hotel had their foundations swept away by the surging Kenwyn river and three large carriages were carried off to pile up against Lemon Bridge. A house occupied by several poor people at the lower end of Goodwives Lane by the Allen river was also swept away, but luckily no lives were lost. Part of the Old Bridge, further down the river, was washed away and horses, in danger of drowning, could only be released from their stables by rescuers on horseback.

Too little water could also bring problems when fires caused havoc in the town. In September 1854 a fire broke out in the premises of Mr Netherton, the bookseller, in Lower Lemon Street. The fire was quenched by neighbours who rushed to the scene and no fire engine was needed, which was just as well, because as the *Gazette* stated, there was a "total want of water in the gutters".

A week later there was another fire which was far more devastating, and only the lack of wind and a full tide prevented an even worse disaster. This started in the premises of a grocer's shop by the West Bridge, one of a small group of three-storey buildings which stood where cars now park in Victoria Square. "The flames spread with lightning rapidity and in a quarter of an hour the part that first caught was a mass of flame from street to roof." Over an hour later "the whole block was now involved in one vast body of flame, from which vollies *(sic)* of fire-balls like the stars of Roman candles were shot up to a great height, while an occasional light breaking out beyond the limits of the conflagration showed where another house was in danger." The heat from the flames must have been enormous as the ruins smouldered and smoked for several days with small fires breaking out again from time to time. The town fire engines used water from the river, helped by a full tide and the closing of the sluice gates at Lemon Bridge, to prevent the spread of the flames, but it was surprising that no other houses were badly damaged, as this block of four houses had been separated from River Street by a lane only eighteen feet wide, and from Kenwyn Street by an even narrower alley.

Truro had already experienced other spectacular fires earlier in the century. In October 1811 the midnight ringing of the fire-bell alerted Truro people to the flames pouring out of Plummers' skin and woollen workshops in Kenwyn Street, but "by good management and spirited exertions of the people the fire was prevented from spreading." The *Gazette*'s report on this incident included these comments: "We are sorry to hear that Messrs. Plummers' loss exceeded the amount insured," and "a multitude of the working classes laboured with honest zeal in carrying water and justly deserved the thanks of the town and the consideration of the Fire Insurance Companies who profited by their exertions." The front page of the newspaper at this time often carried advertisements from various Insurance Companies who had agents in the town, and events like this would no doubt increase their business.

S U N   F I R E   O F F I C E,

Bank Buildings, and Craig's Court, Charing Cross, LONDON;

For Insuring Houses and other Buildings, Goods, Merchandise, Ships in Harbour, in Dock or building, and Craft, from Loss and Damage by Fire

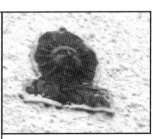

Above: A Sun Fire Office token on a house in Truro

Festivals, Fevers, Fires and Floods

The Plummers suffered from several more fires in the following years, one of the worst being in 1820 when the alarm bell from St Mary's and continued cries of "Fire! Fire!" resounding through the streets woke people from their sleep, as the Spinning Mill by the River Allen behind the church burned "with the utmost fury." The roof fell in and "from the interior of the premises arose a majestic column of fire, on which the power of the engines could not make the slightest impression." This time the Plummers' insurance cover was greater, "so that the circumstances most to be regretted is the loss of time to the industrious work people during the re-erection of the machinery."[10] In the 1840s another disastrous fire, this time in wood-works in Malpas Road, threw nearly a hundred people out of work and showed up the deficiencies of the fire engines, which took an hour to arrive and then the hose was found to be too short to reach the river at low water.[11]

Premises like these were obviously bad fire hazards but there was another danger at these times: gas explosions. A gas works began manufacturing in Truro early in the nineteenth century, one of the first in the country. In May 1822 gas lamps replaced the seal-oil lamps that had shed light, to some extent, on the main streets of the town, and in November St Mary's church was lit by gas only one week later than St Paul's Cathedral. Richard Polwhele wrote a verse in honour of the Gas Company:[12]

> *Truro's morals as well as appearance must show*
> *What praise to your labours and science we owe;*
> *Our streets and our manners you've equally brighten'd,*
> *Since our town is less wick-ed and much more enlighten'd!*

When F.W.L. Stockdale wrote about his *"Excursions through Cornwall"* in 1824 he commented: "The alterations and improvements made of late years at Truro, have certainly given the town a very neat and handsome appearance; the streets being well-paved, watered, and lighted with gas, are more comfortable than in any other town in the county." However, complaints were not slow in coming as to the effectiveness of the new system and over fifty years later, in 1877, there was even talk of reverting to oil lights,

Truro gas-lamp: photo by John James

*A postcard from John James's collection, showing Truro's gas works
in the middle distance, just left of centre*

but as the Gazette commented: "The illumination given out from our gas lamps
is...just enough to make darkness visible, but it is doubtful whether we should
have so much light as this if we get oil lamps."[13] Gas continued to light Truro's
streets for many years to come.

When the fire broke out at West Bridge in 1854 the Gas Company quickly
cut off the supplies to prevent possible explosions, but there could be other
causes of explosions. The fire at Netherton's the previous week had been
started by an explosion in which Mr Netherton's twenty-year-old brother,
William, had been badly burned. Unknown to anyone he had gone to Redruth
that afternoon to buy three pounds of gunpowder and on his return had taken it
to his room at the top of the building with a lighted candle, with dreadful
consequences for himself.

William had been able to travel to Redruth and back that afternoon
much more quickly than in former times, because since August 1852 there had
been a passenger rail link between Truro and Penzance, passing through
Redruth, with five trains a day each way, but as yet there was no rail to connect
Truro with Devon and beyond. Although steam power had been in use in
Cornwall for over one hundred and thirty years and Richard Trevithick had
pioneered its use by engines on rail, and mineral tramways or railways were
being used in Cornwall linking mining areas to ports, Cornwall fell behind

WEST CORNWALL RAILWAY TIME TABLE

Trains will run at the following Times until further notice, Sundays excepted.

Miles.	UP.	MORN. 1	MORN. 2	MORN. 3	AFT. 4	AFT. 5
	Penzance Departure	..	8 40	10 0	12 35	5 0
2	Marazion Road..	..	8 45	10 5	12 40	5 5
6¾	St. Ives Road..	..	8 55	10 15	12 50	5 15
7¼	Hayle	..	9 0	10 20	12 55	5 20
8¾	Angarrack	..	9 5	10 25	1 0	5 25
13¼	Camborne	6 30	9 30	10 50	1 25	5 50
15¼	Carn Brea......	6 35	9 35	10 55	1 30	5 55
10¼	Redruth	6 45	9 45	11 5	1 40	6 5
18¾	Scorrier Gate ..	7 0	10 0	..	1 55	6 20
25	Truro Road (arrival)........	7 25	10 25	..	2 20	6 45

Miles.	DOWN.	MORN. 1	MORN. 2	AFT. 3	AFT. 4
	Truro Road (departure)	7 35	10 40	2 35	7 0
6¼	Scorrier Gate	8 0	11 5	3 0	7 25
8½	Redruth	8 15	11 20	3 15	7 40
9¾	Carn Brea	8 25	11 30	3 25	7 50
11¾	Camborne	8 30	11 35	3 30	7 55
16¼	Angarrack	8 55	12 0	3 55	8 20
17¾	Hayle	9 0	12 5	4 0	8 25
19¼	St. Ives Road	9 5	12 10	4 5	8 30
23	Marazion Road	9 15	12 20	4 15	8 40
25	Penzance (arrival) ..	9 20	12 25	4 20	8 45

A railway timetable published in the West Briton*, 1854. "Truro Road" was the station at Highertown, in use between 1852 and 1855.*

much of the rest of the country during the time of "railway mania", in the 1830s and 1840s, when most of the main rail network of the country was being built. In 1851, when many other people in the country could take advantage of special rail services to make the once-in-a-lifetime visit to London to wonder at the ingenious displays of the Great Exhibition in the amazing creation of the Crystal Palace, Cornish people had to start their journey by slower horse-drawn vehicles, such as William Hodge's Omnibuses, which travelled between Truro and Exeter three times a week, or take the steam packet boat from Hayle to Bristol, in order to catch a train. Cornwall, that had once been in the forefront of the technological changes of the Industrial Revolution, was now being left behind.

Sarah Gregor wrote about the huge improvements to roads in Cornwall during her lifetime especially when the roads were Macadamised (with John Macadam's son acting as surveyor for the improvement of many of the turnpike roads in the area), but she added: "We were left in the lurch, for just as we had learnt to make roads such as our forefathers never dreamt of, the Iron Horse revolutionised the whole system, and while we boasted of our rapid trot, our countrymen were flying under the influence of steam, an advantage for which we sigh in vain."[14]

One of the reasons for this was easy access to water for transport, but there were also the engineering problems and expense in building viaducts over the many deep valleys that cut through the Cornish hills. The editor of the *Gazette* was urging the need for action in 1840 when he wrote: "We may be slow in adopting such improvements...but we must adopt them at last if we would maintain our position among the other counties of England, and save from ruin and decay the important branches of industry which have grown up among us." Falmouth lost its position as a packet station because of this, which must have had its effect on Truro as well. (When a line was finally opened to the port in 1862 it was only a branch line from Truro and not the main line as first envisaged.)

In August 1852, when Truro gained rail communication with Penzance, the station was at first at Highertown until an extension was opened three years later to Newham beside the river. It was to be a further four years before Brunel's bridge over the Tamar finally brought rail communication with Devon. The *Gazette* reported on the progress in the building of this line to Truro, highlighting some of the dangers for the navvies whose brute strength created so much of it. Three accidents were reported in February 1854 alone. In the tunnel being dug at Buck's Head an explosion, caused by sparks falling on loose grains of gunpowder, badly burned two men. Another man fell forty feet from scaffolding in the cutting being made at Bosvigo, injuring his side and ankle. At the partly-built viaduct crossing the Kenwyn at Carvedras close to the smelting works, a rope attached to a derrick used to raise a balk of timber, broke and knocked off one of the men. He saved himself from serious injury or death by grabbing hold of the derrick as he fell. The two great viaducts crossing the Rivers Kenwyn and Allen, with their sturdy stone pillars and fan-like wooden supports holding up the rails, must have been a magnet for Truro people as they watched their building and then marvelled at the first trial train which trundled across them high up over the valleys on 11 April 1859.

The first offical train reached Truro on 3 May, the day after Prince Albert had formally opened Brunel's great bridge across the Tamar. "Nothing

TRURO — *from Trennick Lane.*

could exceed the hearty welcome with which the arrival of the train was greeted", wrote William Pease of Boconnoc. "The town seemed full of people. A procession was formed from the Station to the Town Hall, within the Council Chamber of which the Mayor had provided a splendid dinner to which I had tickets. Champagne was most abundant. We returned by the 6.15 train to Lostwithiel delighted with the day and thankful for having been spared to see the opening of the Cornwall Railway."[15] This line with its thirty-four viaducts was yet another example of Victorian ingenuity and technique, the Truro structures rising higher than any of the other impressive buildings erected in the town during these years.

In November 1862 another bridge was built, a five-arched, stone replacement for the wooden Boscawen Bridge crossing the River Allen, which

Above: part of the 1862 Boscawen Bridge   (Photograph by John James)

Opposite: An engraving, probably dating from the 1850s, showing Brunel's two viaducts spanning the town. The Carvedras smelting works can be seen beside the left-hand viaduct. (Courtesy Cornish Studies Library)

had proved unsuitable. Robert Michell, who had objected to the original bridging, died five weeks later aged ninety three. He had been born when sail and coach were dominant, and had lived to see trains become the new method for transporting both people and goods. Like William Lemon and Thomas Daniell before him he had played his part in many enterprises. He had been chief clerk for Ralph Allen Daniell, then had become a manager for the Hayle company of Sandys, Carne and Vivian, before joining his younger brother William in their own business concerns based in Truro. He had extensive interests in several mines besides East Wheal Rose, and in smelting, with both the lead smelter at Point and the tin smelting works at Calenick. The latter was managed by another brother, John. All ships at the quay flew their flags at half-mast at the news of his death, and on the day of his funeral the shops were partially closed out of respect for this man, whose "integrity and sterling qualities won for him universal esteem and affection", according to the *West Briton*. "The venerable deceased was a liberal subscriber to numerous charitable and benevolent institutions; whatever good he did was done in a quiet, unostentatious way." This included starting and maintaining a school in Point.

An entry for December 1867 in the log book of St Mary's School, which began in Old Bridge Street in the 1840s, records the start of yet another large building in the town. "Holiday in consequence of grand doings in the town today. The foundation stone of the New Public Buildings laid."[16] This "Tudor Gothic" building beside the Green was to replace the Assembly Rooms as the main centre for social activity in the town. Its facilities were to include a large concert hall (the largest room in the county), rooms for the County Library which had been established nearly one hundred years earlier and now contained several thousand volumes, as well as a reading room with newspapers and magazines, and later a Free Public Library was also established there. It included facilities that could be used for activities as diverse as the Truro Philharmonic Society and the Billiards and Chess Society. It also made independent provision for the Freemasons, and housed the Bishop of Exeter's library, the Phillpotts Library, which was given to the clergy of Cornwall in 1856.

School log books of the 1860s and early 1870s, before schooling became compulsory, give some idea of life for poorer people who perhaps would rarely enter the portals of this new building. "Very small school because of the unusually heavy rain", or "Remarkably high tides so that the children from St Clement side unable to pass, the street being full of water",[17] are two of the entries in the log book of St Mary's School. There were many other reasons for a small attendance. How many children today would use as an excuse for

Three details from the Public Buildings: Above and below left, the two entrances to the Bishop Phillpotts Library; below right, Masonic symbol

The original St Mary's School

absence that they could not put on their boots because they were suffering from chilblains? What girls nowadays would plead that Friday being cleaning day they had to stay at home to help their mothers? How many schools today would record: "Smallpox very prevalent in the adjacent streets. Many children at home in consequence"? This was in December 1872 when the epidemic was so bad that three months later it was still raging and no children from infected houses were allowed to attend school. None of the infected children were allowed back until late April. This potentially deadly illness could have been avoided, because the Infirmary had for many years been offering a vaccination service, which was free for poor people.

There were other, pleasanter if unofficial, reasons for absence. "Most of the girls gone maying" was recorded in the register on 1 May 1868. Nearly a year later: "Poor attendance in consequence of a Dancing Bear exhibited in the streets which attracts great attention with the little folk". Circuses arrived in the town regularly and in September 1865, for instance, the log book of the British School in Kenwyn Street recorded: "Smaller attendance in afternoon. Circus in town."[18] Eight months later St Mary's School recorded: "Small school this afternoon owing to a Circus being in the town. Children admitted to the afternoon performance at 1d each." In July 1868 two circuses came in less than a fortnight, and there were many other reasons for absence from St Mary's over the following days, which unlike the British School did not take a holiday in August that year. There was a Foresters' Fair at Tregothnan, a Band of Hope Gala at Tehidy, a Wesleyan Methodist School Treat, a horticultural show in the market hall, a swimming match in the Truro River and yet another circus. Even when children were present they were not always very receptive: "August 4 Very warm weather; children very tiresome."

The Circus Comes to Town - here passing the back of the Red Lion.
An undated photograph, probably early 1900s   (Courtesy RIC)

These schools had regular visits from people connected with their management and interested in the progress of the children. These might sometimes have been regarded as an unwelcome interruption and perhaps it was with some relief that the teacher at St Mary's recorded at the end of one week in September 1871: "No visitor this week." Sometimes their visits brought practical help. Mrs Stokes, probably the wife of Henry Sewell Stokes, poet and Town Councillor, visited the British School in September 1863 when "she was pleased with the order", but also noticed the ragged appearance of one of the boys and sent him some clothes. The Misses Tweedy were also frequent visitors here and on one visit Miss C. Tweedy read to the children, when "the girls were quieter than the boys." The rector of St Mary's church, Henry Bullocke, was a regular visitor to his school and Miss Bullocke often came weekly to give the girls lessons in darning. It is perhaps a little surprising that they did nothing to improve the cleanliness of the building. A new teacher took over in 1874 and reported on her first day: "The school is by no means tidy nor clean and there is a most offensive smell proceeding from the Closet." Six months later the Inspector's report stated: "The room is ill-ventilated and the stench from the bad drainage is intolerable - it is difficult to understand how the managers can have allowed the premises to remain in their present unhealthy state."

This was not the only problem reported by the new teacher. She complained that the girls were "dreadfully behind in numeration" and there were insufficient books so that she had to resort to borrowing from the boys' section of the school which was "very inconvenient". Lessons for the girls here were fairly basic with the emphasis on the "3 Rs", reading, writing and arithmetic, with some needlework and geography, and the learning of the Church Catechism which was very important. Lighting of the schoolroom was obviously inadequate because there were references to the girls practising singing carols on December afternoons because "it was too dark to see their sewing." There was also little room for recreation. The Inspector's report for 1876 showed concern especially for the infants. "The want of a playground is very much felt, for such young children ought not to be confined so many hours."

One entry, in June 1870, might be an indication that all was not well in Truro. "Several children absent on account of their parents' removing furniture today." Families were moving away from the area, perhaps to join the increasing numbers forced into emigration to find work. Truro began to decline in population and prosperity. Wealth that had once poured into the town was beginning to dry up and prospects looked much less rosy. Much of the copper mining had moved eastwards, away from the Truro area, and then in the late 1860s it suffered a devastating slump from which it never recovered. Tin mining continued, but was facing more foreign competition as well as increased expenses, as mines delved deeper underground and production became ever more problematical. In 1861 the population of St Mary's parish was 3,575, its highest for the nineteenth century, but by 1901 it had fallen to 2,443, a loss of nearly one third of its people, and this at a time when the population in the country as a whole was still rising. Kenwyn, with its large mining population, lost about one fifth, dropping from 10,639 in 1861 to 8,567 in 1901.

In the 1840s and 1850s Australia was the goal for some, especially after the discovery of copper in South Australia, and to this area went crucibles from Calenick and engines from the Perran Foundry, and the Burra mining township of Redruth had one street named after Truro.[19] Isaac Latimer, the chief reporter for the *West Briton* from 1837-44 and a friend of Charles Dickens, acted as an emigration agent in Truro, as shown on many posters of the time. In the 1870s New Zealand seemed to be the favourite destination for some Truro families, and there were regular advertisements in the local papers for

Advertisements from the West Briton:

Above:
13th January 1870

Right and below:
25th June 1852

passages here, as well as to America and Australia.

Truro had been a market town from its earliest days and farming began to play a more important part in the economy of the town with the decline in mining. The Truro cattle market had been held in High Cross once a month since 1827,[20] but the numbers of cattle and sheep in the centre of the town had been causing annoyance and its move to Castle Hill was suggested. In spite of the farmers' protests this was done in 1840. By this time the remains of the castle consisted of a mound, overgrown by grass and brambles with a deep hollow in the centre, surrounded by a grass-covered wall.[21] The mound was cut down, leaving a four-foot-high bank all round the edge, from which the cattle penned below could be inspected. Market days doubled in number, with

regular reports on the prices given in the local papers. This remained the site for the cattle market for about a hundred and forty years, and there were probably many young boys living in the Castle Street area who, as one person remembers today, had instructions from parents to shovel up the droppings from horses and cattle for use on their garden plots, as the animals made their slow way up the hill.[22]

The cattle market on Castle Hill
(Photograph by John James)

In 1866, when foot and mouth disease, or cattle smallpox as it was sometimes called, was particularly bad around Truro, all the children of St Mary's school attended a morning service as part of a Day of Humiliation, when prayers were offered to try to end this scourge.

Festivals, Fevers, Fires and Floods

The fairs still provided a market for farmers, although now less important than formerly. Besides the Whitsun Fair and one in March, there were two in the winter: the November fair, often called the Five Weeks Fair, and another in December called the Fortnights Fair. Farming has its prosperous and bad times and the 1870s were proving difficult years, with growing competition from abroad. In 1877 the Whitsun Fair was described as "the 'slowest' known to the oldest inhabitants" with business poor and entertainments fewer than usual. But the following December the second Truro Fat Stock Show, held in the Market House, which was handsomely decorated for the occasion, was better with "the shorthorns being *the* class of the show".

An increasing number of agricultural societies were formed which held shows, where new ideas for feeding the rapidly expanding population by improving crop yields and cattle breeding and by using more efficient machinery, could be publicised. The Royal Cornwall Agricultural Show and the Royal Bath and West Show were sometimes held at Truro, and Truro even had its own agricultural show song, emphasising the entertainment to be had for one and all.

Truro Agricultural Show

Good people all who hear my voice,
You now have reason to rejoice;
For off to Truro you may go,
To see the Agricultural Show

Chorus after each verse:
But don't go kissing the girls you know
At Truro Agricultural Show.

A motley group you will see there,
Fat farmers and their wives so rare;
Their bouncing daughters neat and clean,
With a pork-pie hat and a crinoline.

From Newlyn East and St Columb too,
There's hump-backed Jim and carroty Joe;
And a special train upon the rail
To bring all the thieves from Bodmin Jail.

Festivals, Fevers, Fires and Floods

They've got a band from Plymouth down,
The best that ever was in the town;
And all the gentry will be there:
'Tis almost as pretty at Whitsun Fair.

There's horses, ponies, cows and calves,
For Truro don't do things by halves.
There be Devon bulls, sheep, pigs and geese:
You can see it all for a shilling apiece.

There's things up there that'll make you laugh;
There's a two-legged cow and a nine-legged calf,
A billy-goat that comes from Wales
With sixteen eyes and seventeen tails.

Now all around I hear them say,
"We'll see that show this very day;
So off we go, all in a row
To Truro Agricultural Show."

I'm glad you're come, I see you're here;
There's thousands come from everywhere:
Rich and poor, high and low,
At Truro Agricultural Show.[23]

A greater interest was also being shown in horticulture, the first meeting of the Royal Horticultural Society in Cornwall being held in Truro in 1832, with Richard Polwhele writing:

Admitted to witness a grand Exhibition,
Where all of one mind with no politics grapple,
I am sure we had fruits fit for every condition,
From the cucumber up to the princely pine-apple.[24]

One of the first subscribers to this society was Sir Charles Lemon, who was awarded the Banksian Medal (named after Sir Joseph Banks, the eighteenth century botanist and plant collector, who had accompanied James Cook in his voyage around the world in the *Endeavour*) for his compilation of new plants growing in his gardens at Carclew. He encouraged the interest and knowledge of two of his employees, William and Thomas Lobb, who later travelled the world to obtain new plants to send back to Cornwall. This was the time when varieties of rhododendrons, fuchsias, lupins, hoyas and hypericums and many other now-familiar flowers began to be cultivated, so creating many of the famous Cornish gardens.[25] It was a prospering industry at a time when others were declining.

In 1867 this advertisement appeared in the *Gazette*: *Truro Nursery. James Treseder, Nursery and Seedsman, begs to return his sincere thanks for the very liberal support he has received for the last twenty seven years in the Nursery and Seed trade, and would now like to inform his Customers and the Public generally that he has taken into partnership one of his Sons, who has had many years experience in the above branch both in England and Australia, and that in future the business will be carried on in the name of James Treseder and Son.*[26] This family firm was to remain in Truro until the 1980s.

In 1877 Truro changed its status from borough to city. It seems ironic that at the very time when the county's population was falling the diocese for Cornwall was finally established, one of the arguments for its creation having been the large size of the population. After years of indecision and government indifference an Act of Parliament was finally passed in 1876 creating the Bishopric of Truro. A year later, on 28 August 1877, the *London Gazette* announced:

> *The Queen has been pleased by Letters Patent under the Great Seal of the United Kingdom ... to ordain and declare that the borough of Truro, in the county of Cornwall, shall be a city, and shall be called and styled, 'the City of Truro, in the county of Cornwall'.*

It had not been a foregone conclusion that Truro would be the Cathedral City. Bishop Phillpotts had first proposed the division of his diocese in 1840 and seven years later the Prime Minister stated that if this was necessary a Bishop of Bodmin would be appointed. This immediately started a battle of words between the two towns. Bodmin had been an important religious centre when Cornwall last had had its own bishop in pre-Conquest days; it was also more central and already had a fine church for a Cathedral; it could also be regarded as the county town where the Assizes had been held for many years and where the county prison had been established. To complicate the situation a third town was suggested, St Columb Major, also with a very fine church, and Bishop Phillpotts accepted this idea, but it came to nothing. In the end it

---

Overleaf: Two engravings of Boscawen Street
Left (courtesy Cornish Studies Library), in the early 1850s;
Right (courtesy RIC), in the 1870s, roughly when Truro became a city.

was Truro that was chosen for a number of reasons including being on the main railway line and having three other churches, apart from St Mary's. But further pressure was still needed to make the Government reach a final decision. It was only after a large sum of money had been offered towards the endowment by Lady Rolle, a Cornish woman, that the necessary act was passed and Edward White Benson was appointed as the first Bishop.

Truro traders soon took advantage of their new status, even before it had official sanction from the Queen. A poem appearing in the *Royal Cornwall Gazette* in March 1877 included these verses:

Who has not heard of Truro? the celebrated place!
That for the Cornish Bishop so lately ran a race,
Though Bodmin did press forward, it stood but little chance,
They might as well have stationed the Bishop at Penzance.

Advantages has Truro, the City now to be,
The place most fitly chosen to crown the Cornish see:
A town where local talent has slumbered rather long!
Which now for exhibition conceives a motive strong.

Though rather prematurely, the Truro tradesmen haste
To make fit preparation for City life with taste,
Where City boots are making gigantic letters tell!
While coach builders are taking the City sign as well.

And as you walk through Truro, with its "Cathedral-lane"
"Cathedral luncheon rooms" would your footsteps now detain,
The "City leather warehouse" is ready to provide
New saddles for all horses the Bishop likes to ride.

The siting of the new Cathedral was the subject of many discussions and arguments. Enlarging St Mary's by extending the west end was one suggestion; a new Cathedral high on a hill overlooking the city was another; the complete demolition of St Mary's to redevelop the site was yet another. In the end it was decided to preserve the south aisle of the old church, with its ornately carved stonework of the early sixteenth century, and to attach the new Cathedral to this. This meant building over the old churchyard as well as demolishing a row of houses to the north, including the Rectory and the Bear Inn, which stretched to the east of the old Assembly Rooms. There was strong feeling from many Truronians about the fate of their ancient church. When surveys of the site were being carried out the people who gathered to watch were sometimes hostile as James Bubb, the Clerk of Works, discovered on one occasion when he set up his theodolite in Old Bridge Street to the accompaniment of abuse thrown at him.[27] The last Sunday evening service to be held there, on 10 October 1880, was full with people standing in the aisles and crowding at the door. The following morning the last marriage ceremony was performed, and as the bridal party left the workmen moved in to start demolition. One of the oldest landmarks in Truro was now to be superseded. The grander building replacing it had already begun five months earlier amidst great ceremony and excitement.

By dawn on Thursday 20 May 1880, horse-drawn carriages of all descriptions were bowling along the roads into the city, filled with excited people who gazed with admiration at the magnificent triumphal arches that spanned the main roads. "Welcome" was blazoned in gold above a wide arch over Boscawen Bridge. "Commerce", "Peace", and "Plenty", were the optimistic words which greeted sightseers coming from Falmouth, as they reached the top of Lemon Street, to pass under a Gothic-style arch over thirty feet high bearing the coat of arms of the new city. At the bottom of the hill the road crossing Lemon Bridge was made narrower than usual by another tall arch, painted to look like marble, with flags fluttering above it and pairs of Corinthian-style columns flanking each side, decorated with urns filled with flowers and greenery, instead of the statuary that had originally been envisaged.[28]

Early trains disgorged more crowds who came by rail to the station on Richmond Hill, where a Moorish-style arch with "Welcome One and All" greeted them. As they poured down the hill and along River Street they passed under a battlemented arch with four round turrets, decorated with coats of arms and the words "Fish, tin and copper". This Cornish Arch and all the other four had been designed by the architect, Silvanus Trevail, for one of the grandest occasions that Truro had witnessed: the laying of the foundation stone of Truro Cathedral by the heir to the throne and Duke of Cornwall, Prince Edward. Most of the arches bore messages of greeting to him such as "Welcome to England's Hope and Pride", and "Welcome to England's Prince" and "God Bless our Duke and Duchess", for his wife was also accompanying him. The message over Lemon Bridge, "Hail Grand Master", was an acknowledgement not only that the Prince was the most important member of the order of Freemasons but that the local members were to play a significant part in this ceremony of foundation.

THE MASONIC ARCH. TRURO.
(ROYAL VISIT, 1880.)
SILVANUS TREVAIL, ARCHT

Festivals, Fevers, Fires and Floods

Truro people were up and about early giving last-minute touches to the colourful decorations, for flags and drapery brightened houses, and shops and other businesses put on special displays. Gills, the draper in Boscawen Street, was transformed by shrubs and evergreens; another draper's shop, Messrs. Andrews and Co., was festooned with the words "God Bless the Prince of Wales" surrounded by flags, the Red Lion was covered with flags, drapery and evergreens, and not to be outdone the Royal Hotel, once Pearce's Hotel and now renamed following a short visit by Prince Albert in 1846, was decorated with a large star as well as fluttering flags. The Town Hall had flags and artificial flowers festooned between the flagpoles which were decorated with painted shields, rich cloth was draped artistically across the frontage and the entrance was be-flagged, as were all the walls inside the market hall.

No doubt last-minute checks were being made here to ensure that the rooms set aside for the royal couple, especially furnished for the occasion by the town's two chief furniture makers and upholsterers, Julians, and Criddle and Smith, were in perfect order, that the raised platform at the far end of the large hall was properly covered in crimson cloth and the two carved and gilded state chairs for the royal visitors had no speck of dust, that the crimson cloth covering the columns was firmly attached and the tables were decorated with fresh flowers and evergreens. Mr John Cooper Furniss would no doubt be checking that all was well in hand for the special luncheon that he was organising for the guests once the main ceremony of the day was over.

The sides of the roads were soon filled with hundreds of people hoping for a share of the excitement and a glimpse of the important visitors through the ranks of soldiers that lined the streets. Nearly three hundred Metropolitan Policemen, brought down from London on a special train the previous evening, also kept an eye on the good-natured crowd. All traffic was stopped at ten o'clock, by which time some of the important men, many of them resplendent in colourful uniforms, were assembling at the Town Hall, including the Mayor, Mr Philip Protheroe Smith; the High Sheriff, Mr C. Prideaux-Brune; and the Hon T. Agar-Robartes of Lanhydrock, whose family had particularly long connections with the city. Then the carriages began arriving from Tregothnan, where the royal couple had been staying, first those of the Earl and other dignitaries, and then, soon after 11.30, the royal carriage with the Prince and Princess and their two sons, George and Albert, flanked by trotting outriders, was cheered into the city. As they arrived outside the Town Hall the National

---

Anthem was played and the main ceremonies got under way.

Speeches of welcome were followed by a ride to Southleigh at the top of Lemon Street, which was lined from top to bottom with mounted men organised by James Henderson, a civil and mining engineer, who had come to live in Truro in 1855, and whose father had often told him of the time he had carried dispatches from the Duke of Wellington up steep Calenick Hill on his way through Truro. From Southleigh the Prince marched to High Cross in a solemn masonic procession. Outside St Mary's church, where there were colourful tents, a grandstand and decorated enclosures, bands played, choirs sang and the robed clergy greeted him. There he laid the foundation stone, checked it with a plumb line and level and then scattered corn and poured wine and oil over it before it was blessed by the bishop. A granite memorial stone was also laid and the High Sheriff presented a purse for the Cathedral funds to the two

The Duke of Cornwall, Prince Edward,
lays the foundation stone of Truro Cathedral, 20th May 1880

Princes containing money from Miss Gurney in memory of her father Sir Goldsworthy Gurney, who had been educated at Truro Grammar School under Thomas Hogg and who had died at his home in Bude five years earlier. His inventions had lit, warmed and ventilated the House of Commons, had helped stop the spread of cholera in London and had improved ventilation in coal mines. He had also tried to establish regular steam carriage services by road, but had met with too much opposition. Eighteen other purses were presented to the Princess by a line of ladies, including one carried by the new Bishop's youngest daughter, Maggie Benson. Her older sister, Nellie, had been busy collecting more money from the crowds, along with twenty-five other young ladies. It was then time for luncheon and yet more speeches.

The day was not yet over. A military review at Treliske, the home of William Teague, a miner who had made a fortune, was on the afternoon's agenda. To reach this house on the hill to the west of the town, the Prince rode his black charger through the streets wearing the uniform of a colonel of the Royal Cornwall Rangers' Militia, with his wife and children following some distance behind in a carriage. In Ferris Town he was confronted by an elephant. This belonged to Wombwell's Circus which visited Truro regularly, and the animal was used to pull a gilded carriage bearing a band, which immediately began to play the opening bars of the National Anthem followed by "God Bless the Prince of Wales." The review at Treliske passed off well, the royal party "did Capt. Teague the honour of entering his mansion and partaking of tea." From there they drove back through the city, and as they left for Tregothnan a royal salute from the Artillery Volunteers echoed through the streets.

For Truro people there was more entertainment. A promenade concert was held at High Cross that evening given by a military band, and after dark the town was lit by special illuminations, which made the streets a blaze of light for the throngs of people still filling the city, the "crystal devices" of Criddle and Smith being the most admired. To round off the day fireworks lit up the night sky from Poltisco, including some showing medallions of the Prince and Princess. As the special edition of the *West Briton* stated: "It is a circumstance notable and satisfactory that the foundation stones of the first Protestant Cathedral erected in England since the Reformation are laid by the Heir-Apparent to the British Throne. It is also peculiarly 'fit and proper' that the stones commencing the building of the Cornish Cathedral should be laid by the Duke of Cornwall."

References

[1] Stockdale, S.W.L., *Excursions through Cornwall 1824*, D. Bradford Barton, 1972

[2] Truro Buildings Research Group, 1985

[3] *Robson's Commercial Directory of Cornwall*, 1840

[4] Polwhele, 1803-8

[5] *Royal Cornwall Gazette*, 12 November 1847

[6] Douch, 1977

[7] *Royal Cornwall Gazette*, 3 May 1839

[8] *Royal Cornwall Gazette*, 12 November 1847

[9] Maber, R. & Tregoning, A. (eds.), *Kilvert's Cornish Diary*, Alison Hodge, 1989

[10] *Royal Cornwall Gazette*, 23 July 1820

[11] Douch, 1977

[12] Polwhele, 1826

[13] *Royal Cornwall Gazette*, 22 June 1877

[14] Hawkridge, C., "Sarah Gregor of Trewarthenick", JRIC 1969

[15] Woodfin, R.J., *The Cornwall Railway*, D. Bradford Barton, 1972

[16] Log Book for St Mary's School, 1866-95, CRO (SR/TRU-5/1)

[17] ibid.

[18] Log Book for the British School, 1863-97, CRO (SR/TRU-1/1)

[19] Payton, 1996

[20] Douch, 1977

[21] Whitley, H.M., "Notes on the History of Truro", JRIC X

[22] Personal communication by David Brannlund

[23] Personal communication by Richard Lingham

[24] Polwhele, 1836

[25] West, 1990

[26] *Royal Cornwall Gazette*, 7 February 1867

[27] Brown, 1991

[28] *West Briton* special edition 21 May 1880

Afterword

"Surely Truro doesn't have much history," commented someone to me.

I hope that the preceding pages will have dispelled that idea, especially as the one book originally envisaged has insisted on expanding to two volumes, and even then much will inevitably have been omitted. The twentieth century is the only one that can be dealt with through many personal memories, and as these have accumulated I came to realise that they deserved a separate book in order to do them justice.

The laying of the foundation stone of the Cathedral in 1880 seemed an appropriate point at which to end the first volume, as this building has dominated the city within the memory of everyone born and brought up in Truro in the succeeding years.

Bibliography

Barton, Bradford, *Essays in Cornish Mining History*, Vol.2, D. Bradford Barton, 1971

Beresford, Maurice, *New Towns of the Middle Ages*, Alan Sutton, 1988

Boyan & Lamb, *Francis Tregian, Cornish Recusant*, Sheed & Ward, 1955

Brown, H. Miles, *The Story of Truro Cathedral*, Tor Mark Press, 1991

Bullock, F.W., *A History of the Parish Church of St Mary, Truro,* Jordan, 1948

Burton, E., *The Georgians at Home*, Longmans, 1967

Coate, Mary, *Cornwall in the Great Civil War*, D. Bradford Barton, 1963

Davidson, R.E., *The History of Truro Grammar School*, Kingston, 1970

Dorling, T.J., *The Silver Ship of Truro*, Author, 1982

Douch, H.L., *The Book of Truro*, Barracuda, 1977

Duffin, Anne, *Faction and Faith*, University of Exeter Press, 1996

Elliott-Binns, L.E., *Medieval Cornwall*, Methuen & Co., 1955

Gibson, A. (ed.), *Early Tours in Devon and Cornwall*, A.M. Kelly, 1968

Griffiths, J., *The Third Man*, Andre Deutsch, 1992

Halliday, F.E., *A History of Cornwall*, Duckworth, 1959

Hatcher, J., *Rural Economy and Society in the Duchy of Cornwall 1300-1500*, CUP, 1970

Henderson, Charles, *Essays in Cornish History*, first published 1935, re-published D. Bradford Barton, 1963

Jenkin, A.K. Hamilton, *The Cornish Miner*, George Allen & Unwin, 1927

Jenkin, A.K. Hamilton, *News from Cornwall*, Westaway, 1951

Johns, Charles, *Pendennis Headland, the Defences, 1540-1956*, Cornwall Archaeological Unit, 1992

Keast, J. (ed.), *The Travels of Peter Mundy*, Dyllansow Truran, 1984

McGrady, Richard, *Music and Musicians in Eighteenth Century Cornwall*, University of Exeter Press, 1991

Noall, C., *A History of Cornish Mail Coaches*, D. Bradford Barton, 1963

Palmer, June, *Truro in the Seventeenth Century*, Author, 1989

Palmer, June, *Truro in the Eighteenth Century*, Author, 1990

Palmer, June (ed.), *Truro During the Napoleonic Wars*, June Palmer, 1992

Payton, Philip, *Cornwall*, Alexander Associates, 1996

Pearse, J., *The Wesleys in Cornwall*, D. Bradford Barton, 1964

Pearse, R., *The Ports and Harbours of Cornwall*, H.E. Warne, 1963

Pennington, Robert, *Stannary Law*, David & Charles, 1973

Polsue, Joseph, *Parochial History of the County of Cornwall*, first
        published, W. Lake, 1867-73, re-published E.P. Publishing
        Ltd., 1974

Polwhele, Richard, *The History of Cornwall*, first published 1803-8,
        re-published Kohler & Coombes, 1978

Polwhele, Richard, *Traditions and Recollections*, 1826

Polwhele, Richard, *Biographical Sketches in Cornwall*, 1831

Polwhele, Richard, *Reminiscences in Prose and Verse*, 1836

Rea, Joan, "The Great Mr Lemon at Home", *History Around the Fal*, Part
        V, Fal Local History Group, 1990

Rowse, A.L., *Tudor Cornwall*, first published 1941, re-published Dyllansow
        Truran, no date

Sheppard, Peter, *The Historic Towns of Cornwall*, Cornwall Archaeological
        Unit, 1980

Spreadbury, I. (ed.), *1795 - Through Cornwall by Coach*, 1971

Tregellas, Walter, *Cornish Worthies*, Elliot Stock, 1894

Truro Buildings Research Group publications:

        The Princes Street Area, 1978

        Boscawen Street Area, 1980

        Pydar Street and High Cross, 1981

        Lemon Street and its Neighbourhood, 1983

        River Street and its Neighbourhood, 1985

        From Moresk Road to Malpas, 1988

West, Joan, "A Study of the Cornish Plant Hunters", *History Around the
        Fal*, Part V, Fal Local History Group, 1990

Whetter, James, *Cornwall in the Seventeenth Century*, Lodenek Press, 1974

Wicks, A. (ed.), *Bellum Civile, Sir Ralph Hopton's Memoirs*, Partizan
        Press, 1988

Index

Italics indicate illustrations or maps.

Other Landfall Books
relating to Truro

High Days: Truro High School Celebrates by **Viv Acton (1996), £3.00**
1996 marked the centenary of Truro High School's present school building. This fully illustrated book gathers together memories and achievements of pupils over the decades, and it thus presents much information of general interest regarding the City.

The Bells of Truro by **Phyllis M. Jones (1994), £4.95**
Phyllis Jones (*née* Rule) was born and brought up in Truro, attending Truro County School for Girls during the 1930s. After a period working in the Truro branch of Lloyd's Bank she trained as a nurse at the Royal Cornwall Infirmary. She now lives in Wales, where she is well known as a writer of poetry, short stories, a prizewinning novel and autobiographical works. In *The Bells of Truro* she remembers her Cornish childhood and teenage years, often dominated by the chiming of the bells of the Cathedral and the town clock.
   Illustrated with atmospheric sketches by Truro artist Derek Jenkins.

The Landfall Book of Truro by **Bob Acton (1990), £1.25**
This 16-page booklet includes street maps and indices, together with brief details of five walks - four of them in the surrounding countryside and one consisting of a "historical walkabout" in the City itself.
   Bob is currently (1997-8) working on a successor to it, which will be very much more detailed and will be closely related to information contained in Viv's *History of Truro*. Publication is planned for the period immediately following publication of Volume 2 of the *History*.

Walks in and around Truro are included in three other books by Bob Acton: ***Around the Fal*** (£3.99), ***A Second View from Carn Marth*** (£4.95) and ***Exploring Cornwall's Tramway Trails*** Volume 2 (£6.99).

For an up-to-date list of Cornish titles published by Landfall, write to
Landfall Publications, Landfall, Penpol, Devoran,
Truro, Cornwall TR3 6NW
or ring (01872) 862581.